Vortex Over Wave

#ElasticBandPhotos

Sue Finch

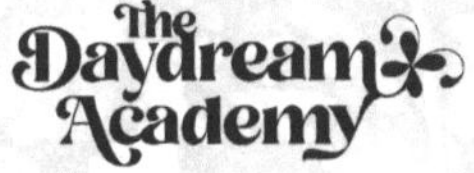

The Daydream Academy

Vortext Over Wave
by Sue Finch
Copyright © 2023 by Sue Finch

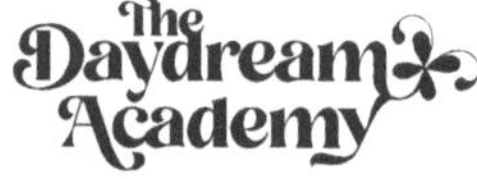

Published in the UK by The Daydream Academy 2023
55 Parliament Street, Stroud, England. ST5 1JW.
www.thedaydreamacademy.com

ISBN 978-1-916680-00-5 (paperback)

A CIP catalogue record for this title is available from the British Library

Designed and edited by Jason Conway, The Daydream Academy.
Photography by Sue Finch

**For Kath, the woman who always walks with me. Thank you for your unending
enthusiasm about what it is I see.**

Hugest thanks to Jason for helping to bring this book into the world. Thanks must also go to my
family for always being encouraging, and to Beth, Cicely, Jo, Jude, Julie, Julie, Kev, Lisa, Lyn, Maria,
Marian, Matt, Merril, Nina, Roger, Robert, Sarah, Sue and all those who have supported my elastic
band photos and joined in. Here's to all the future finders of #ElasticBandPhotos.

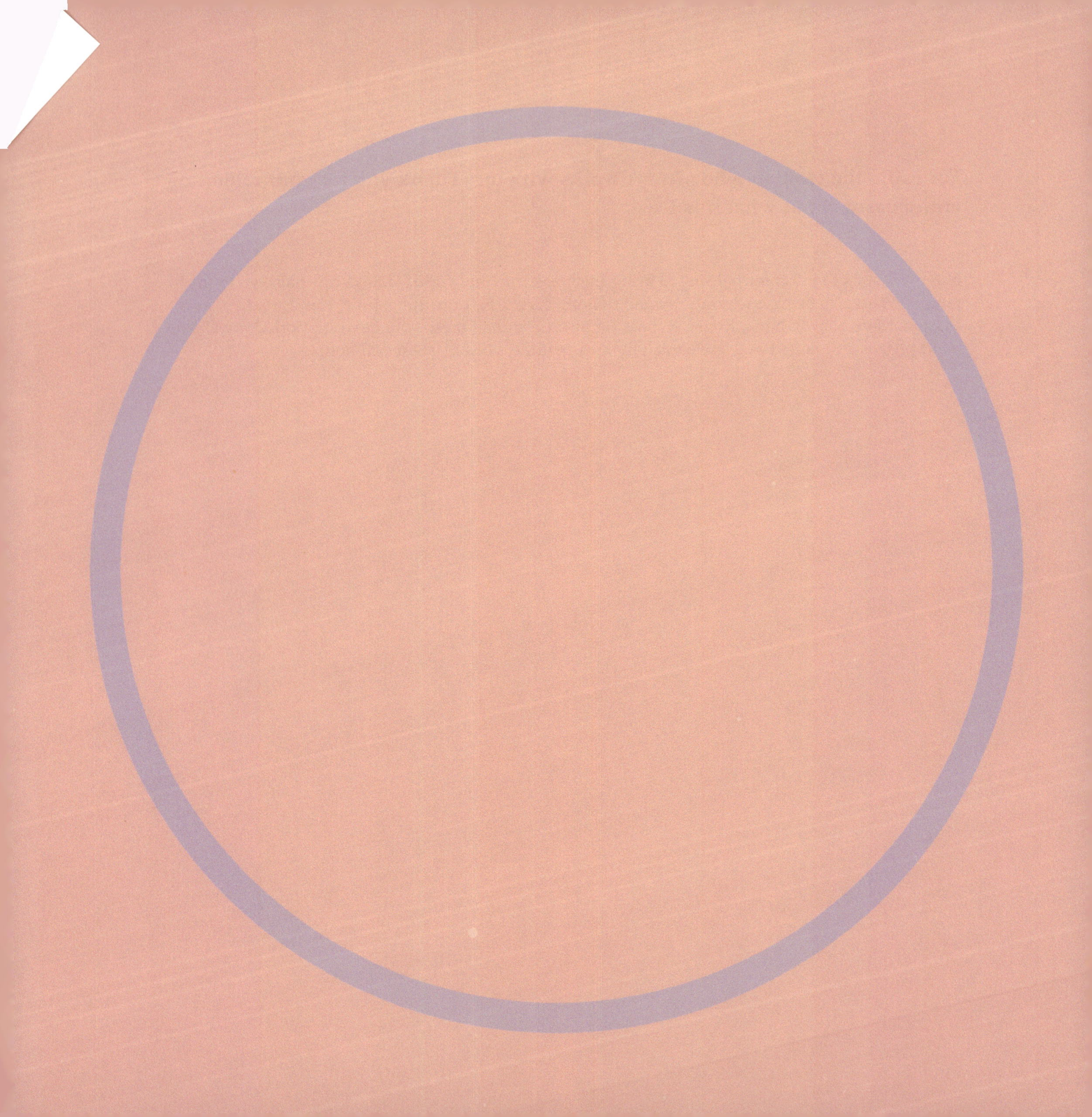

Contents

Introduction

It all began in 2021 when I saw an elastic band on the ground and to me it looked like a treble clef. I photographed it, gave it the title 'Variation on a Treble Clef in Shadow', and posted it on social media. Later that year on one of my daily walks I saw a shoelace that looked like an elephant hawk moth caterpillar, and then a little further down the road an elastic band resembling the mirror image of a six which I called 'Not a Roll of the Die'.

I then seemed to notice elastic bands quite often whilst out on walks, and I loved the way my snapshots could turn them into something more than discarded rubber bands. The challenge I set myself was to create the title for each photograph in the time it took to capture the image and edit it to a square photo on my phone.

I loved finding the bands in places where they would not be expected, such as The Great Orme and Loggerheads Country Park.

A couple of friends started to notice my elastic band photos and commented on them positively. One friend took a trip to Australia to see her daughters and sent me a photograph of a purple elastic band, which became 'In a Puddle by the Laundry Shed in the Garden'. The connection across the miles was wonderful and the colour in these photos contrasted well with the greyer images I was photographing in Wales.

In the same way as finding the detail in the little things by tweeting something I noticed on the way to work each morning during lockdown, these photographs gave me a focus for finding something unique within an ordinary moment in time. There is a marking of time within them that is matched by the poems written for each full moon of 2022. I love the fact that these photographs and poems have now been set down in a book.

I AM HOWLING TO JANUARY'S WOLF MOON

by this I mean I have no words
by this I mean I am too tired to speak
by this I mean I think if I started, I wouldn't stop
by this I mean there is too much I am holding in
by this I mean I am struggling
by this I mean I need to ask for help
by this I mean I need you to help me
by this I mean please howl at the moon with me
by this I mean I need you not to be scared

by this I mean I am terrified.

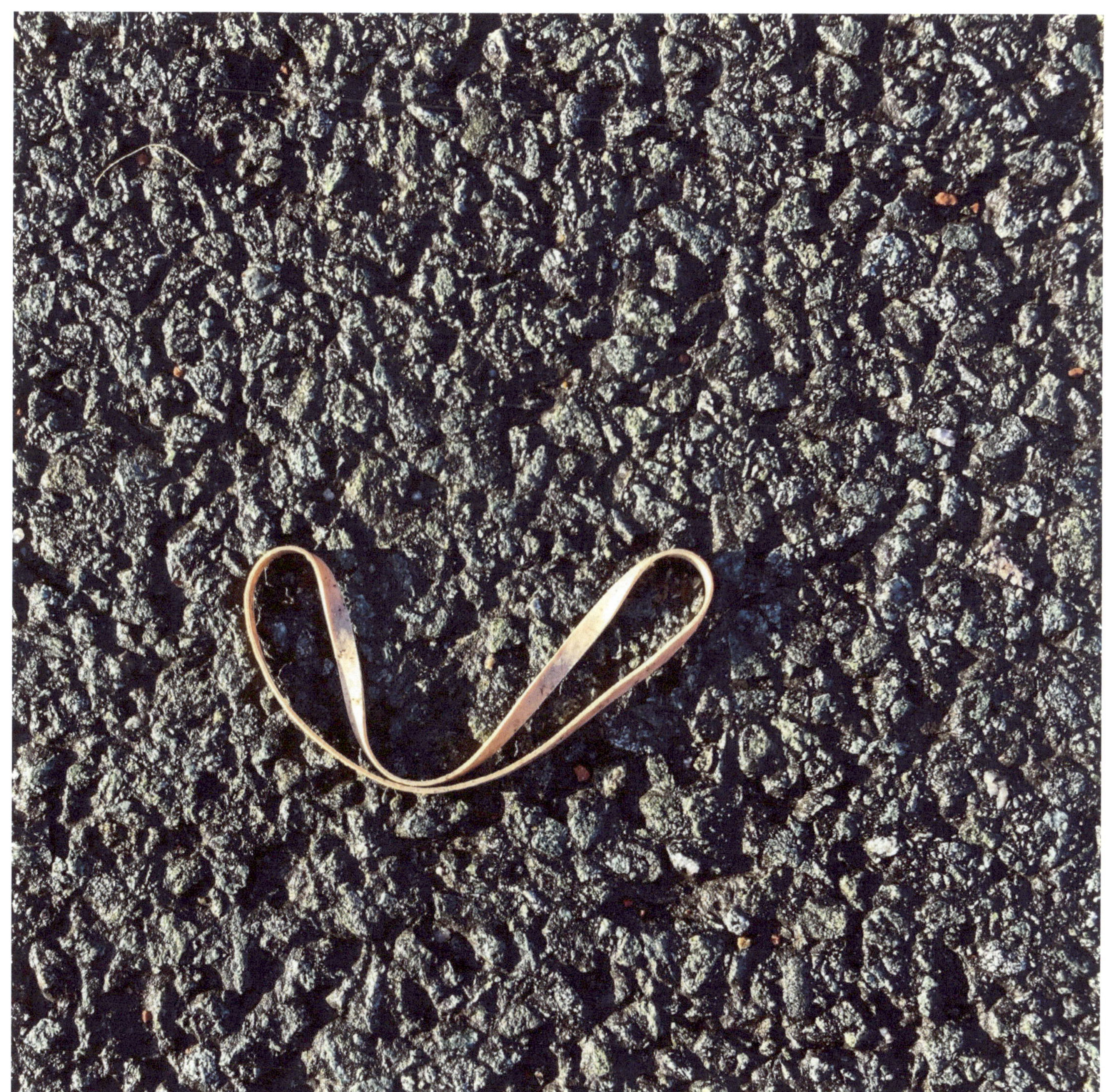

Wry Smile

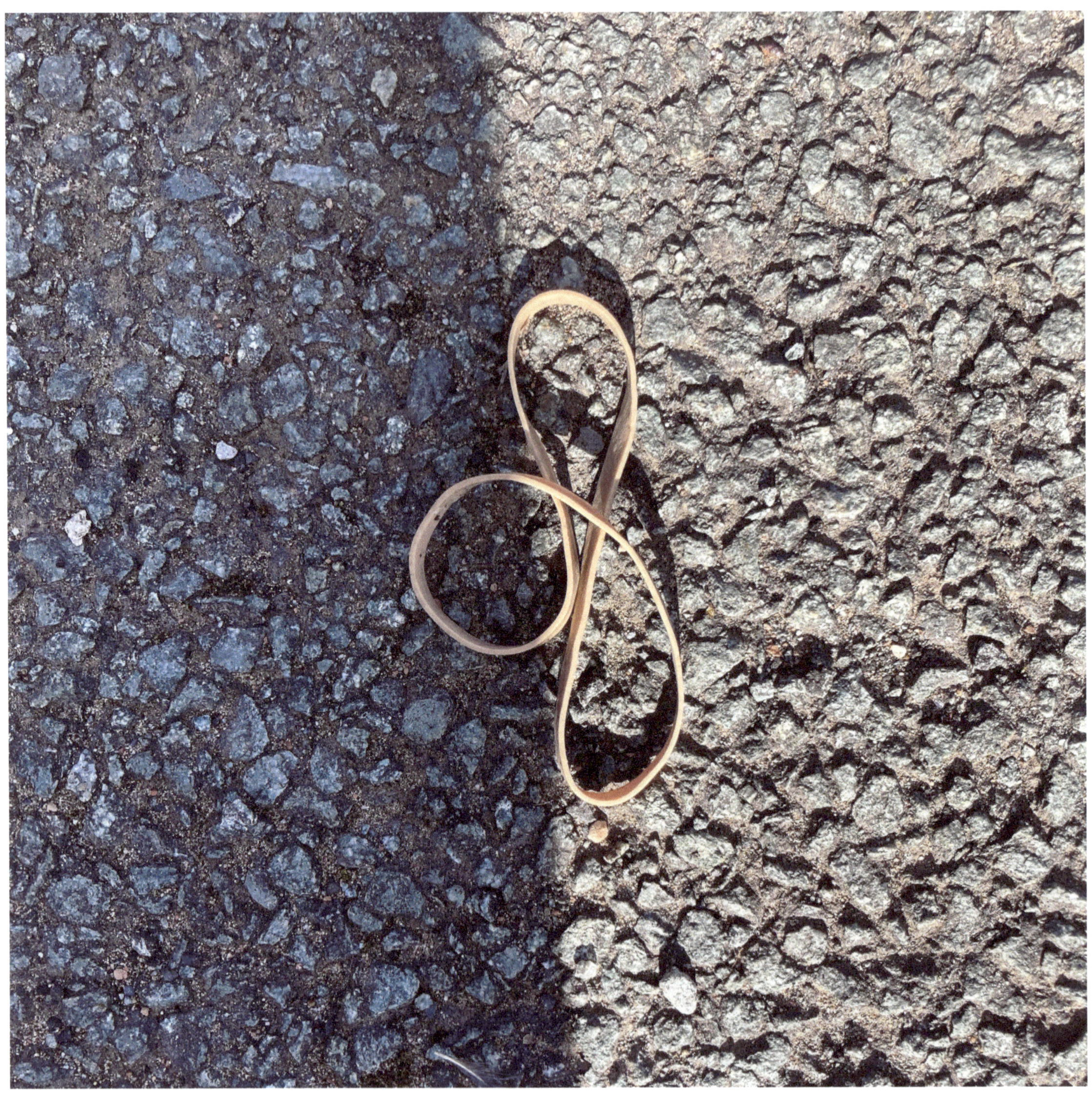

Variation on a Treble Clef in Shadow

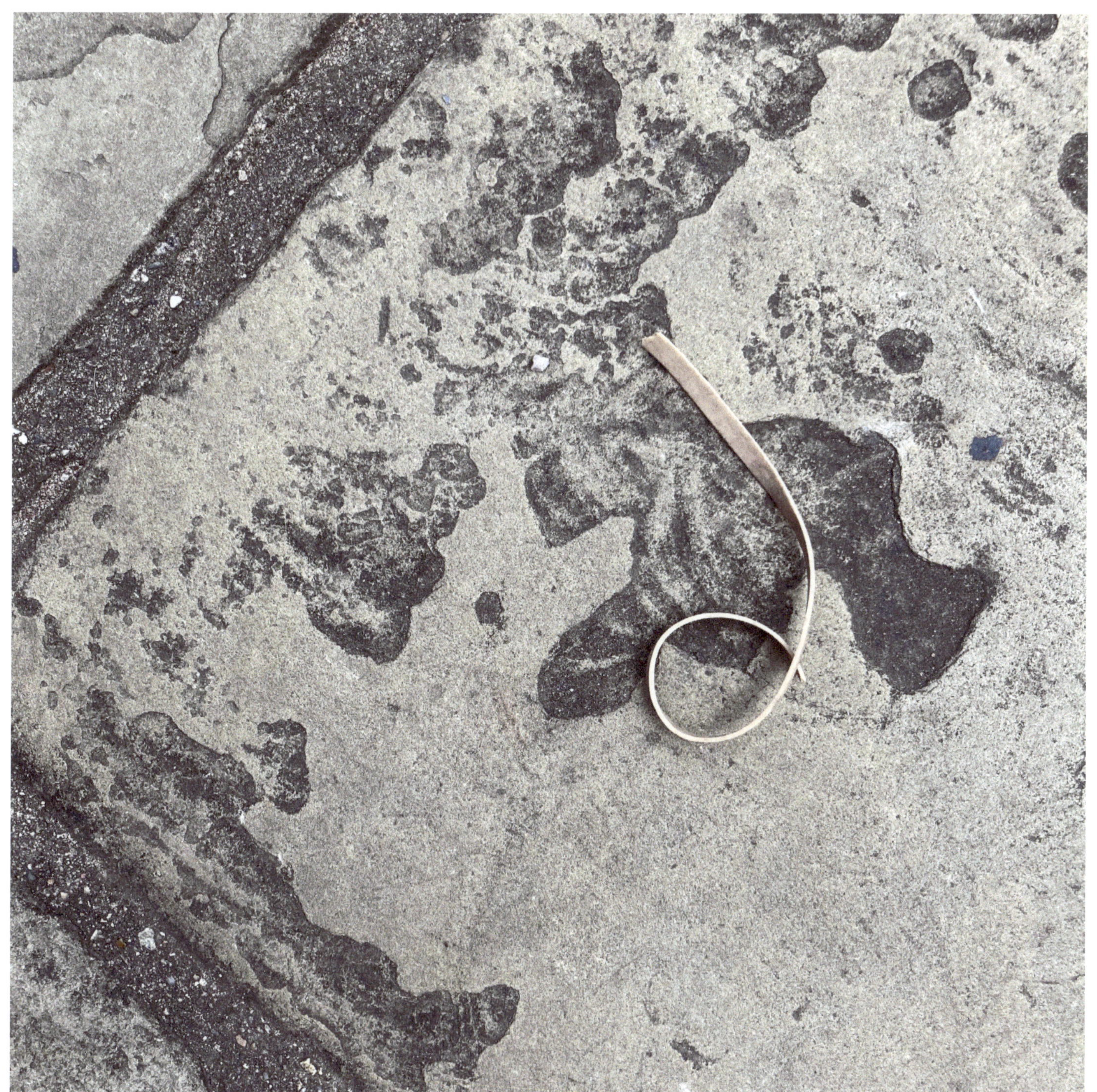

Not a Roll of the Die

SNOW MOON

For a moment this morning I called you
Tiger Moon.
You let the clouds stripe you before first light.

On my way home you hung low over fields
then winked at me in my rear-view mirror.

When I asked your real name
you whispered *Snow Moon*

and the storm winds blew wild.

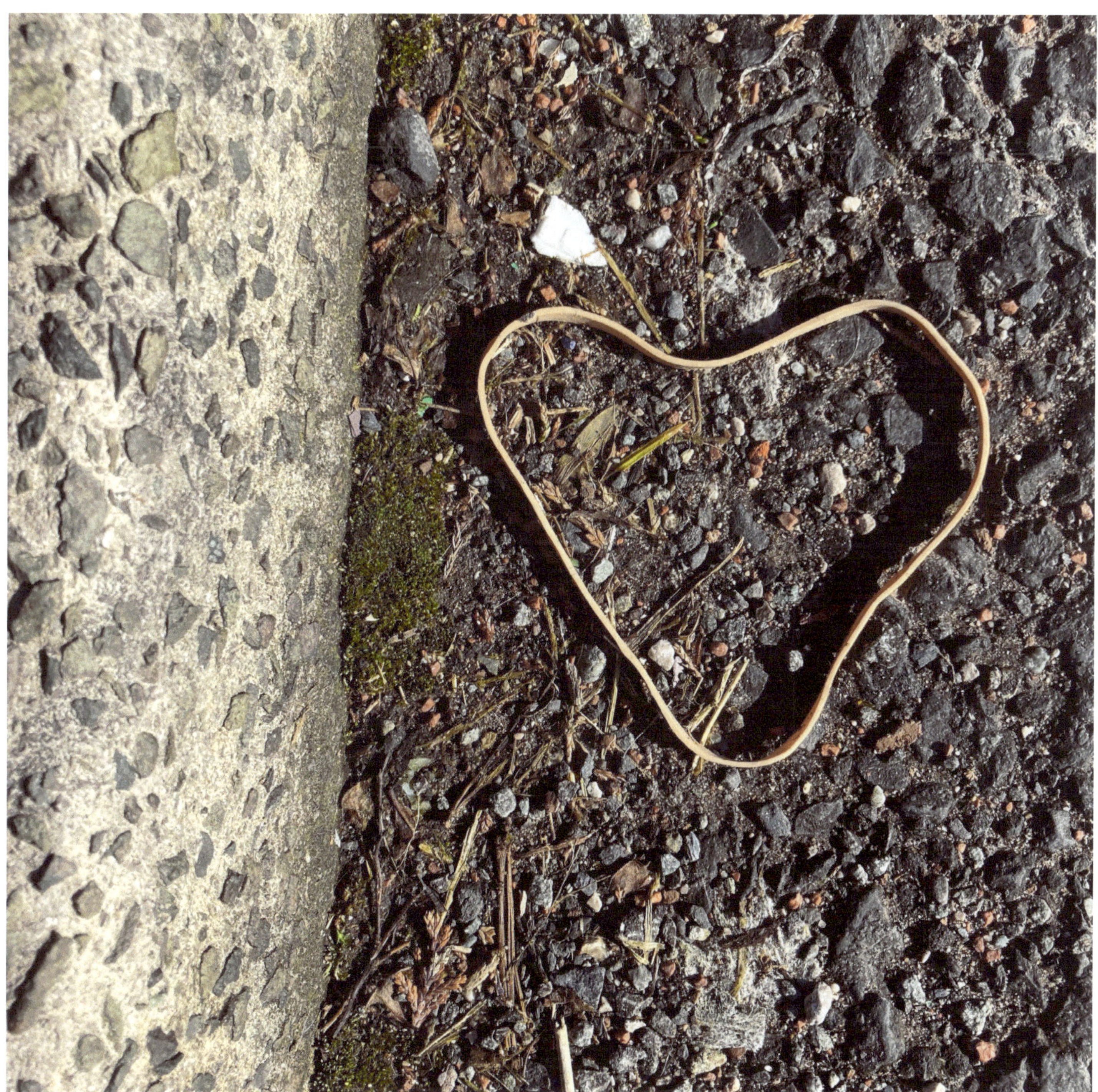

Lovely

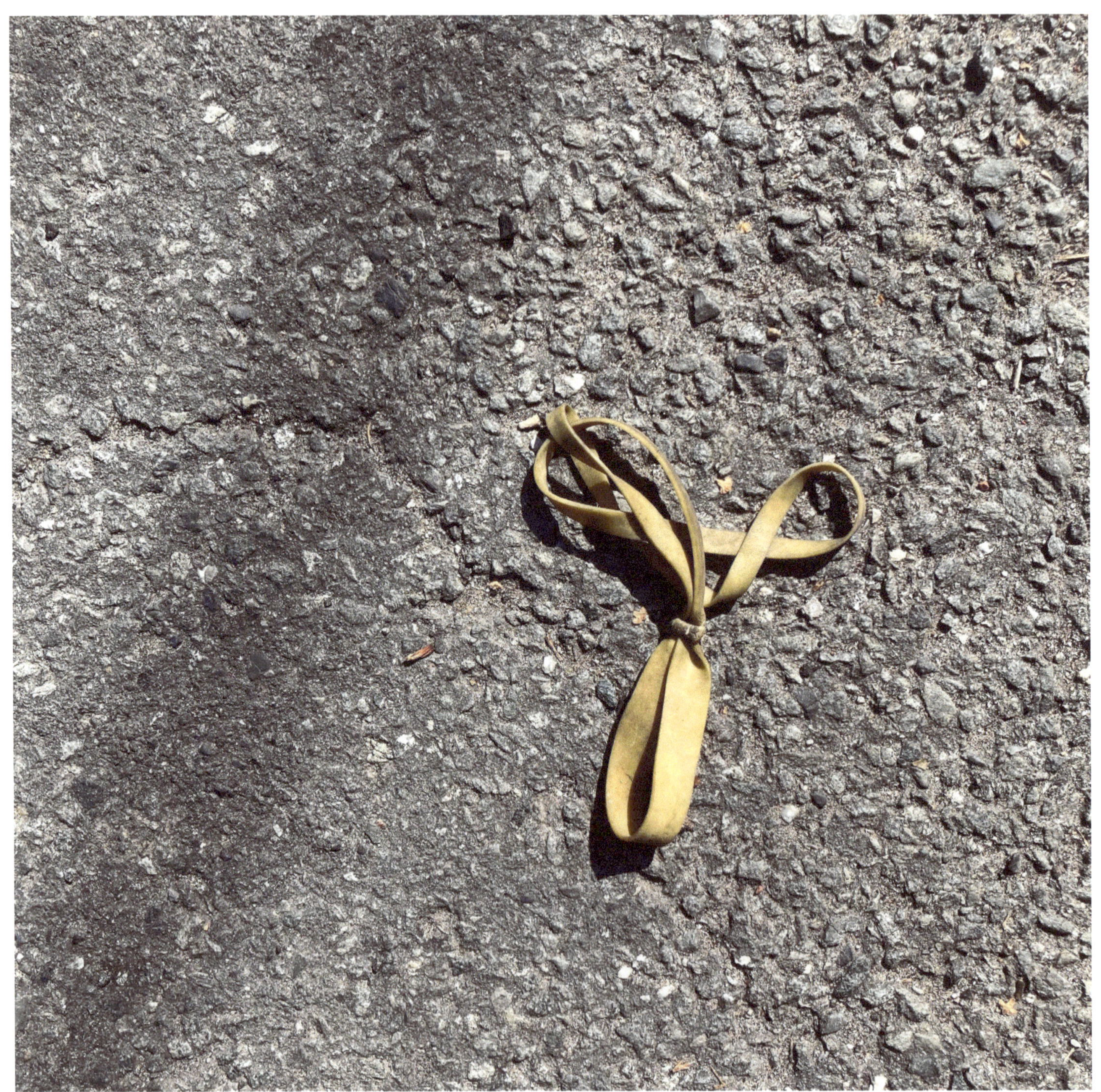

14

Catapult

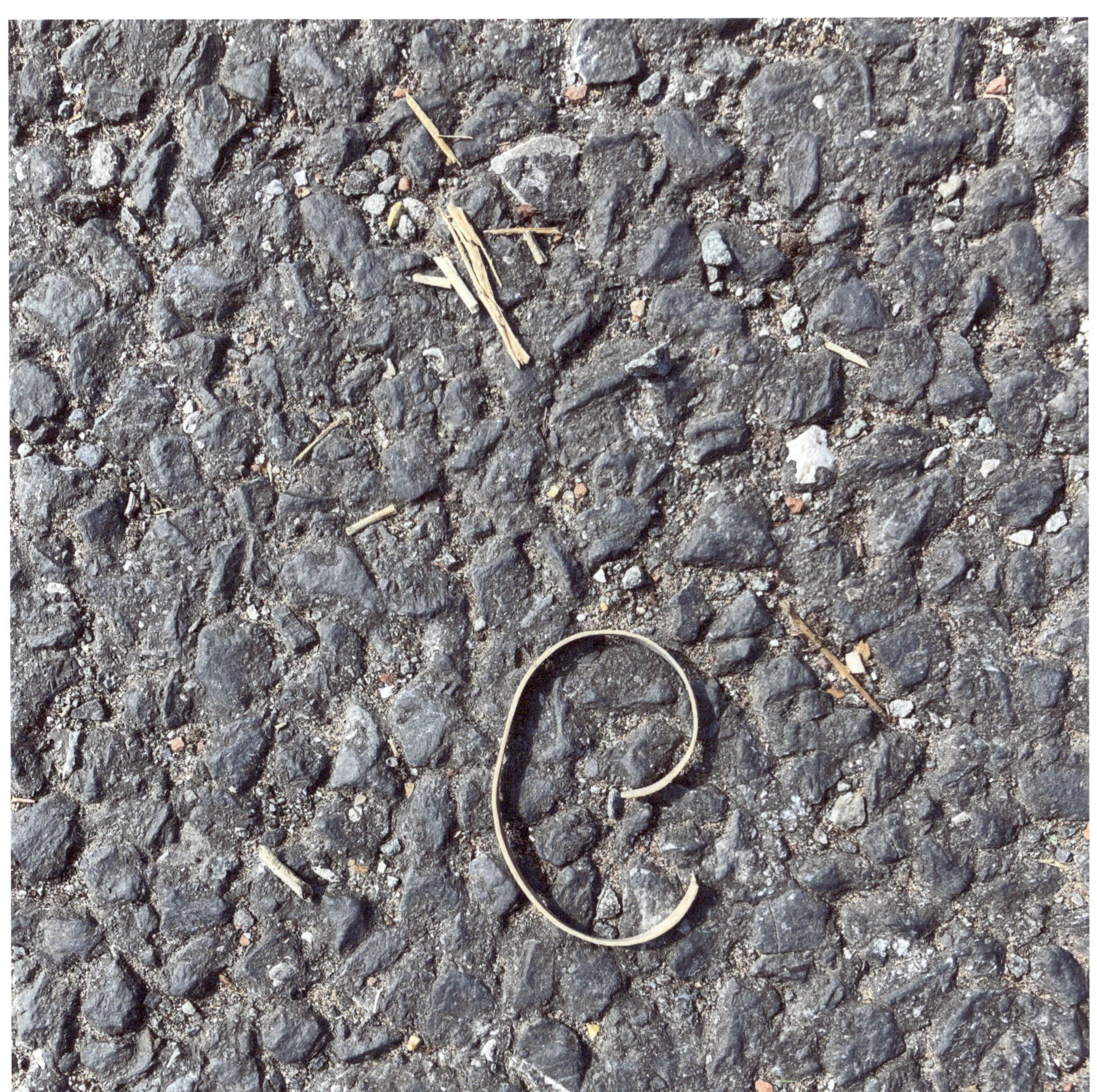

Ear

THEY CALL IT WORM

And it could be named
after a blackbird's feast
or beetle larvae.
Either way spring is soon.

Yesterday, when I rang you,
as I do most days on the way home,
it was behind me.

I asked you if it was full.

You said you couldn't see it yet
so I told you I was holding it
safely in my sight.

Kneeling on the bed to draw the curtains,
you saw it right in front of you
between the trees

proof that I was heading
in exactly the right direction.

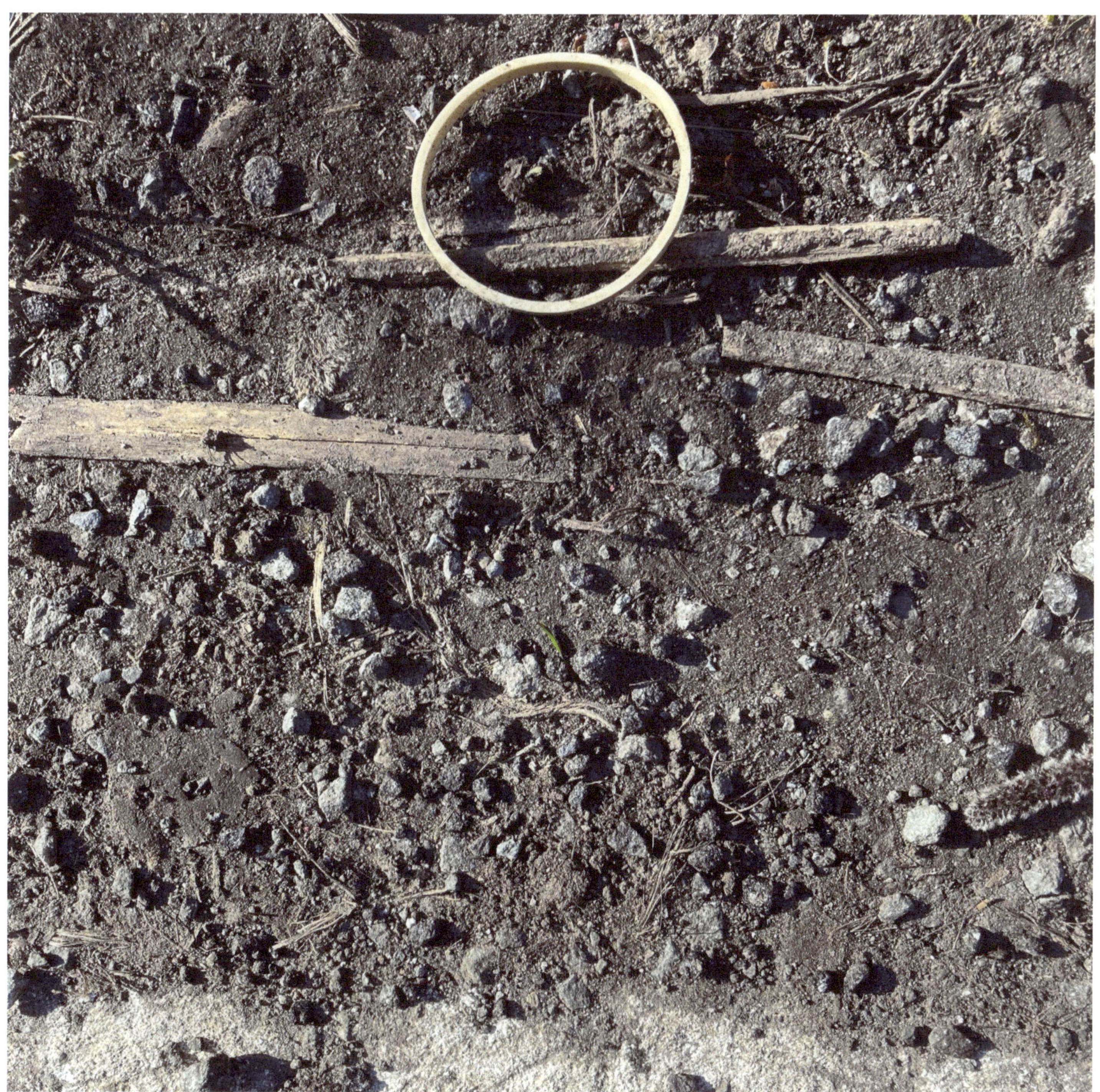

Fallen Circle

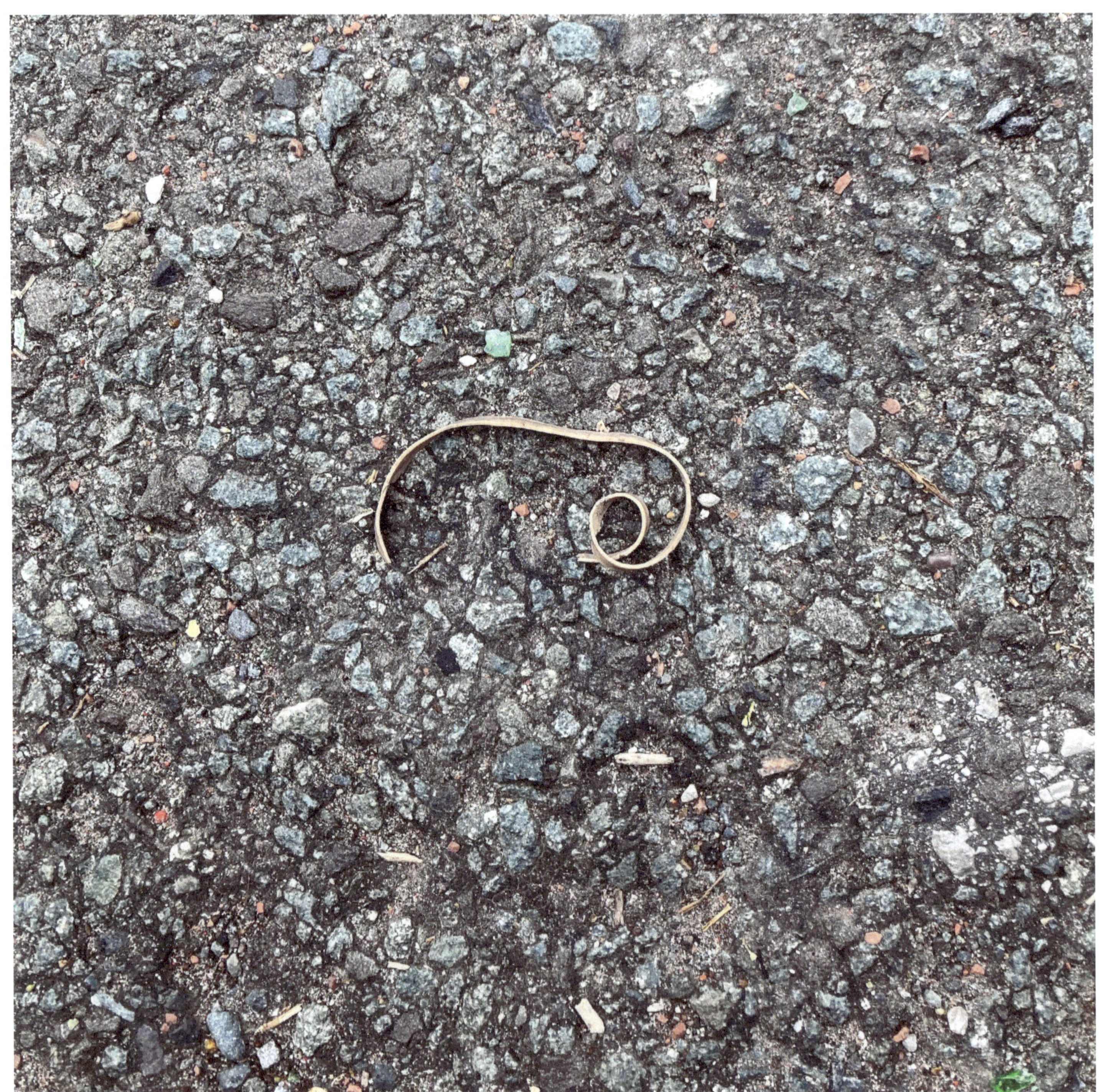

Elephant

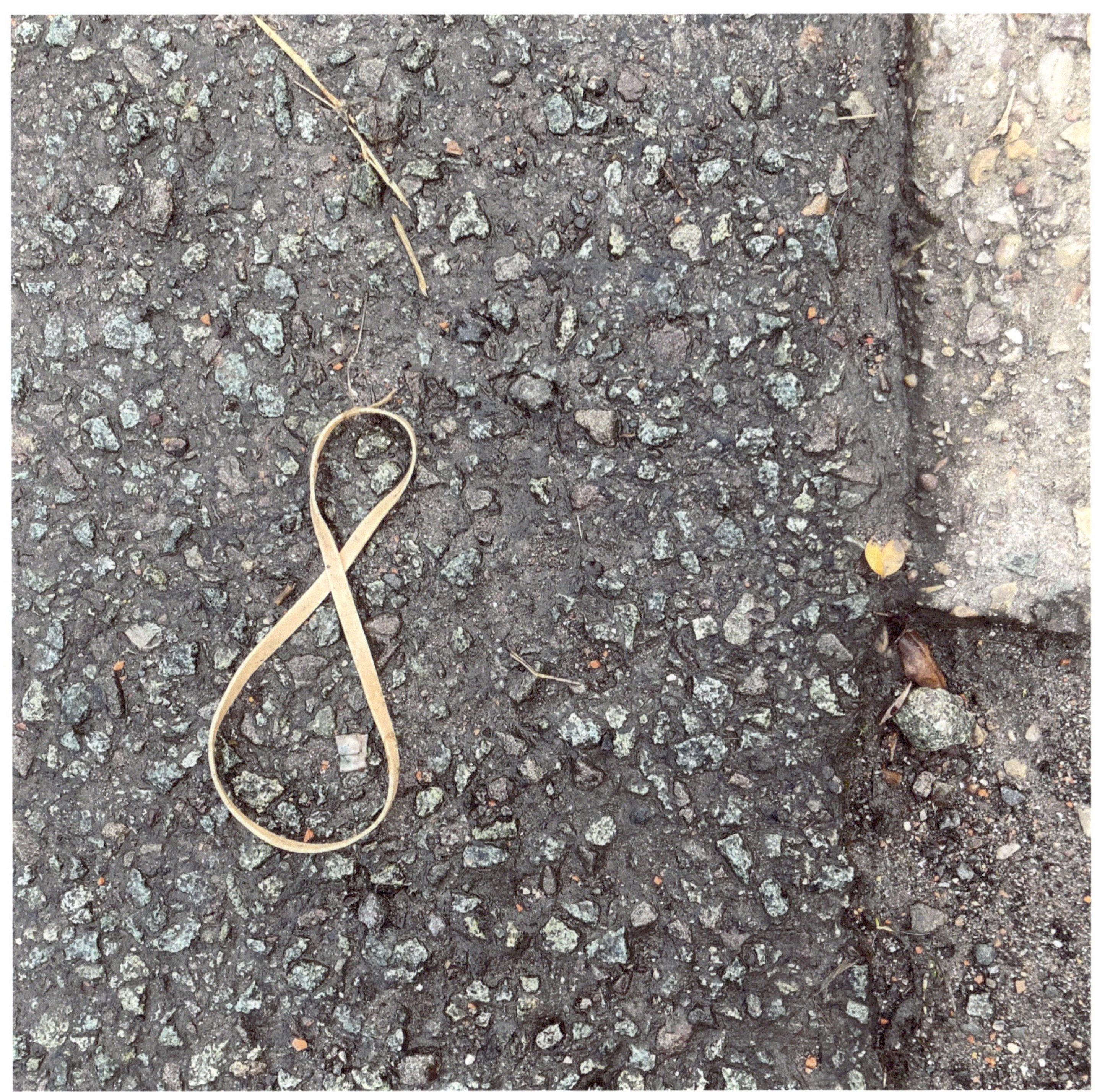

Twist

IT IS GOING TO BE PINK

When I was little
the flowers my mum called *pinks*
seemed just like carnations to me.
But I quietly trusted
that they were something else.

Now I wonder what flowered first
after all those ferns,
that backdrop of only green.
Did anyone ever call ancient gorse
'thorned yellows'?

I run through the colours of the rainbow
for flowers. Find violet.
I must remember to tell her
of the marvel of them appearing
in the shade of the rosemary.

I have never really gone for pinks;
I am more purples, oranges.
But April's full moon is coming
and suddenly I long for an eastern horizon
and a field of phlox.

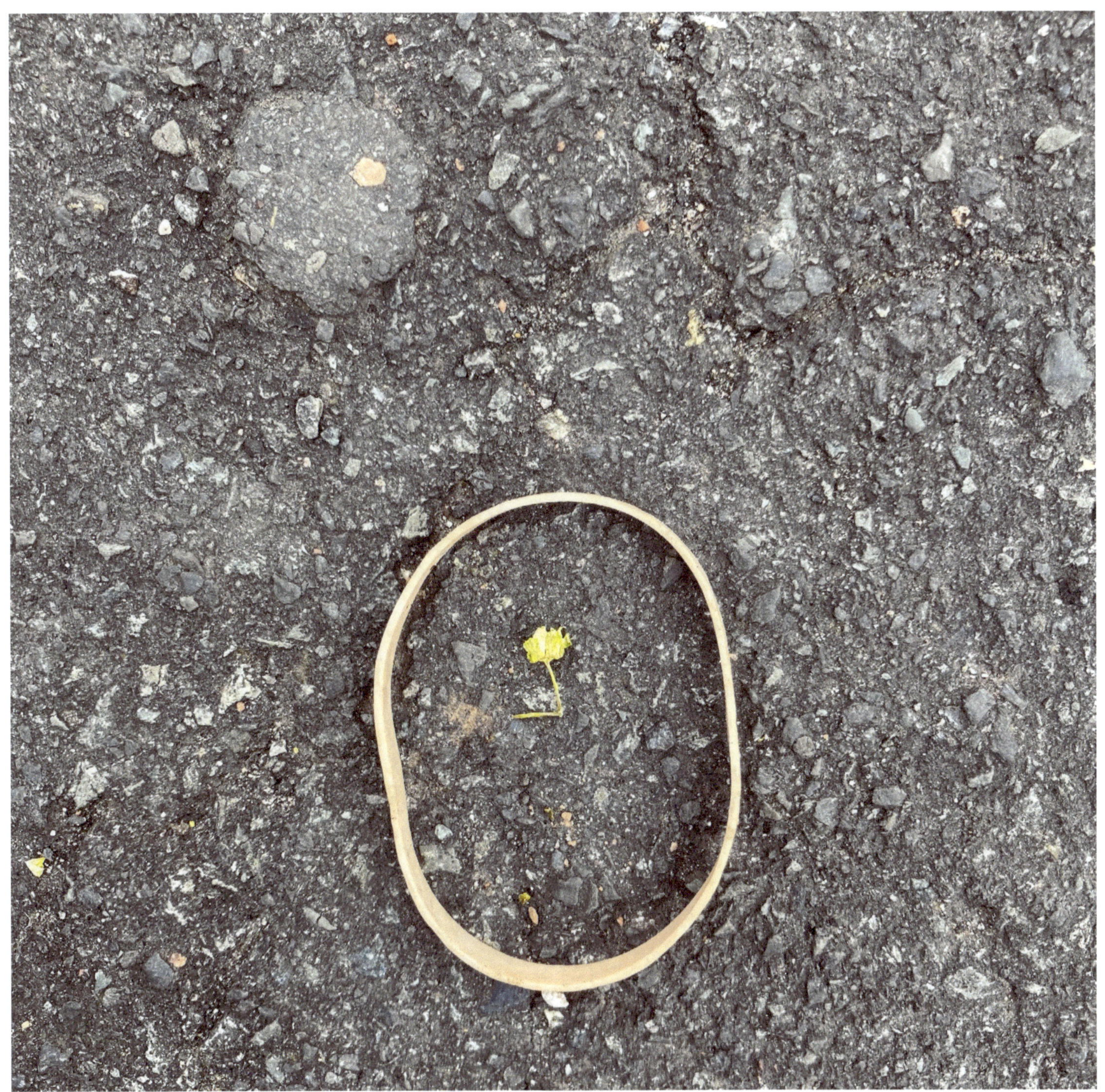

Full Moon Over Flower

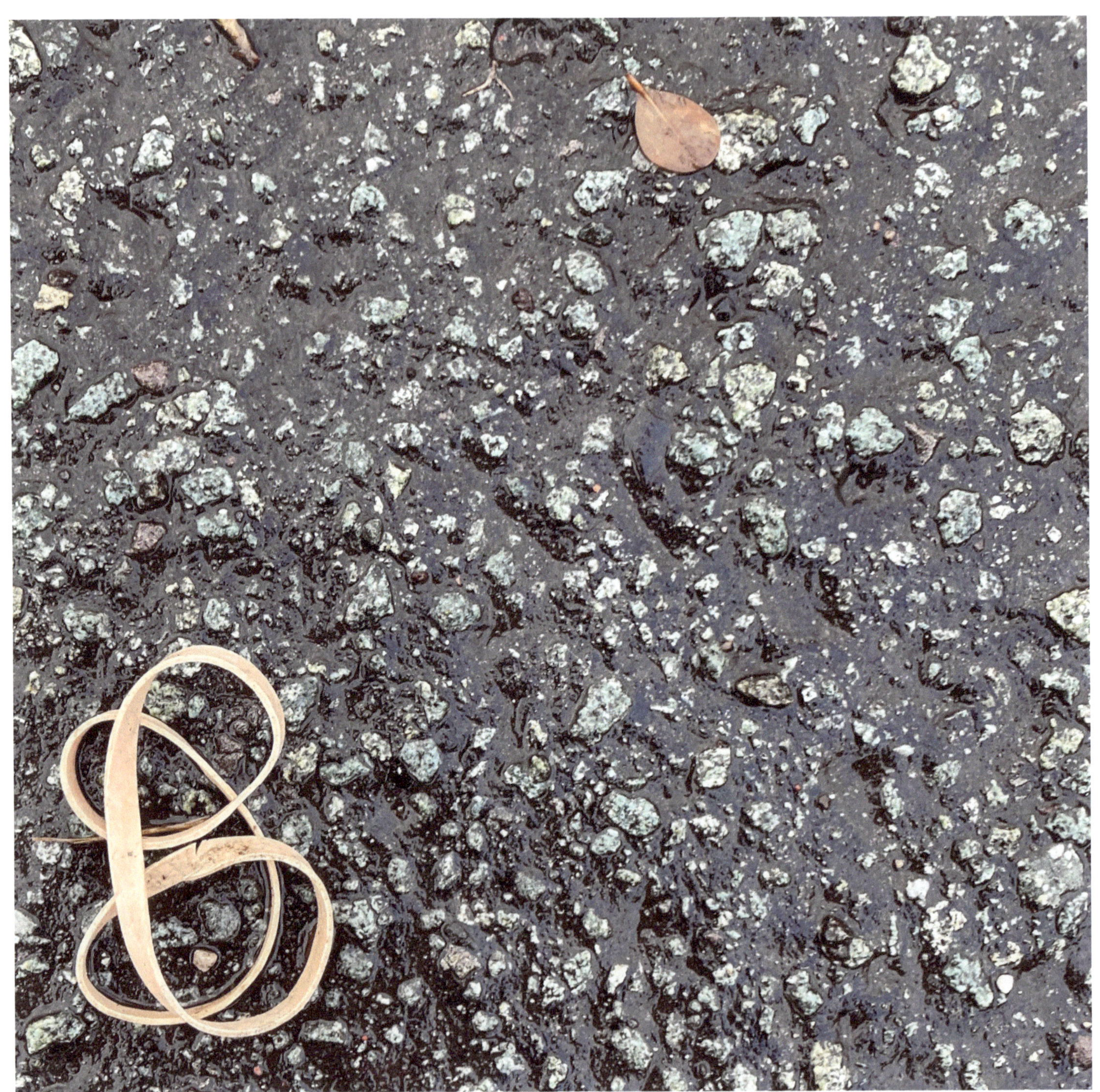

Back to Back B

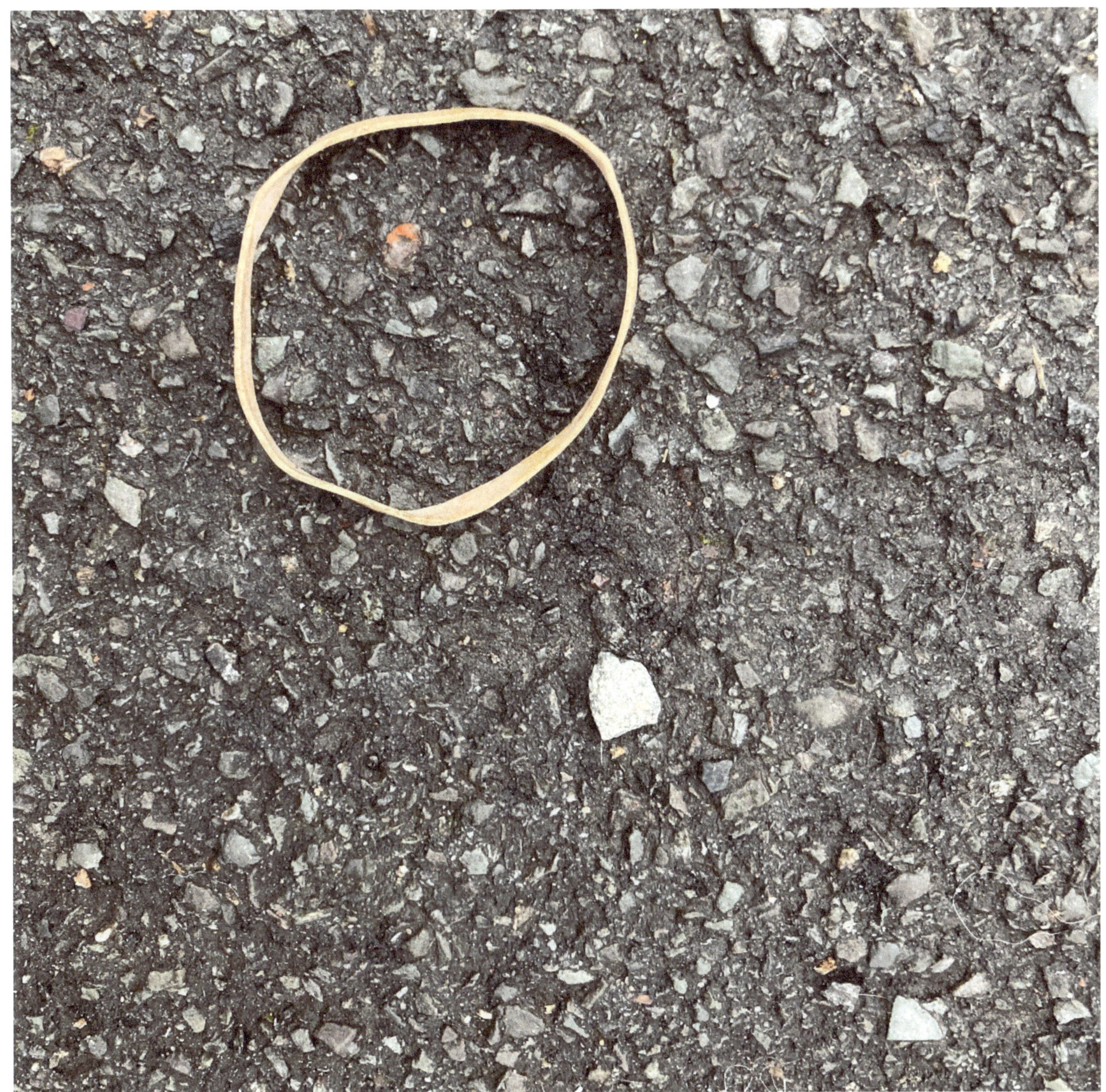

Thought Bubble

FLOWER MOON

You wait until the sky is midnight-blue
then pull on a pair of black corduroy flares.
Flowers appear from hem to waist
as you fasten the zip.
Blousy petals
in vibrant purples, oranges and pinks.
Flower Moon you are laughing and dancing.
And I am here longing
to hear your song.

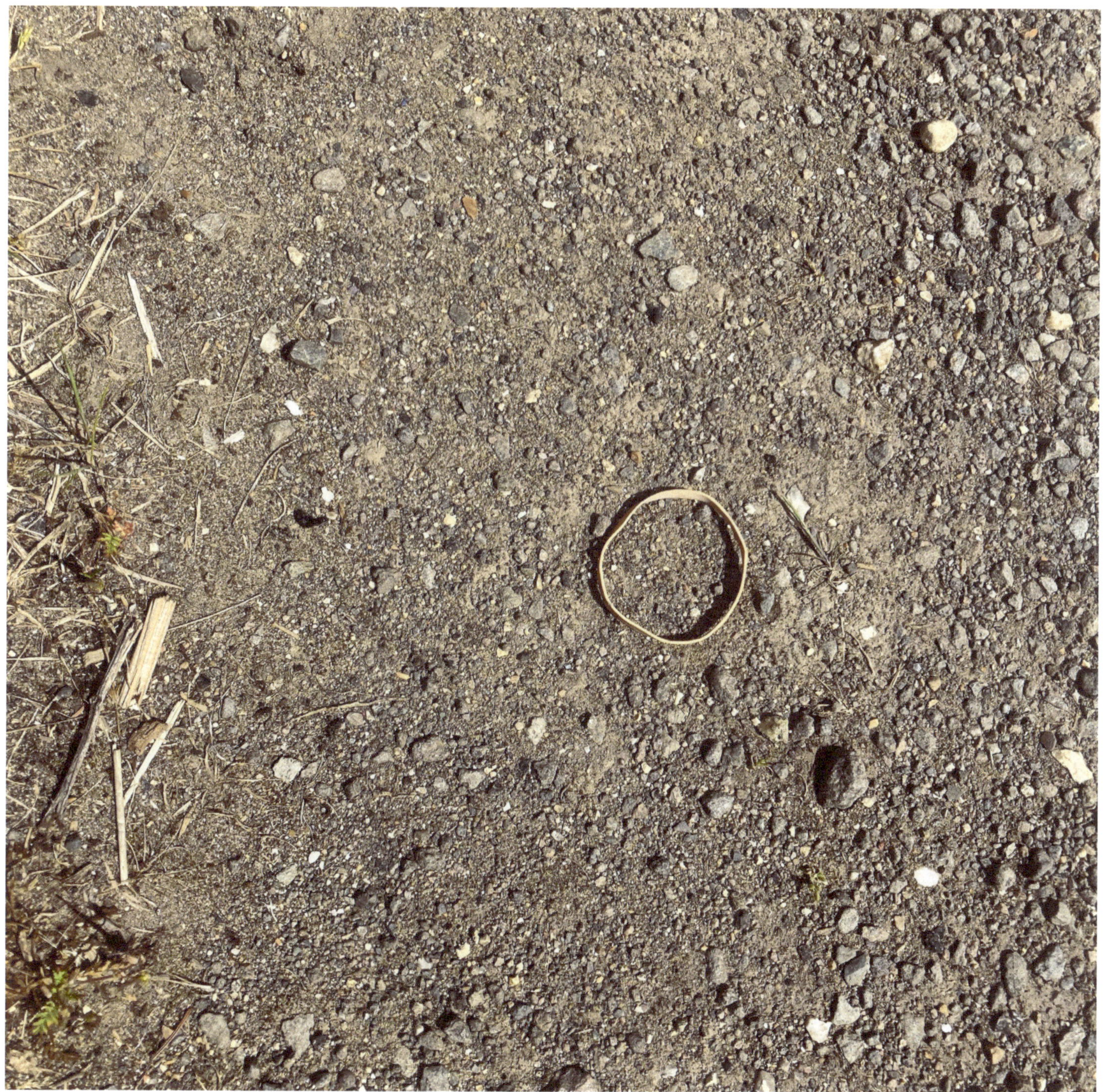

Weedon Bec

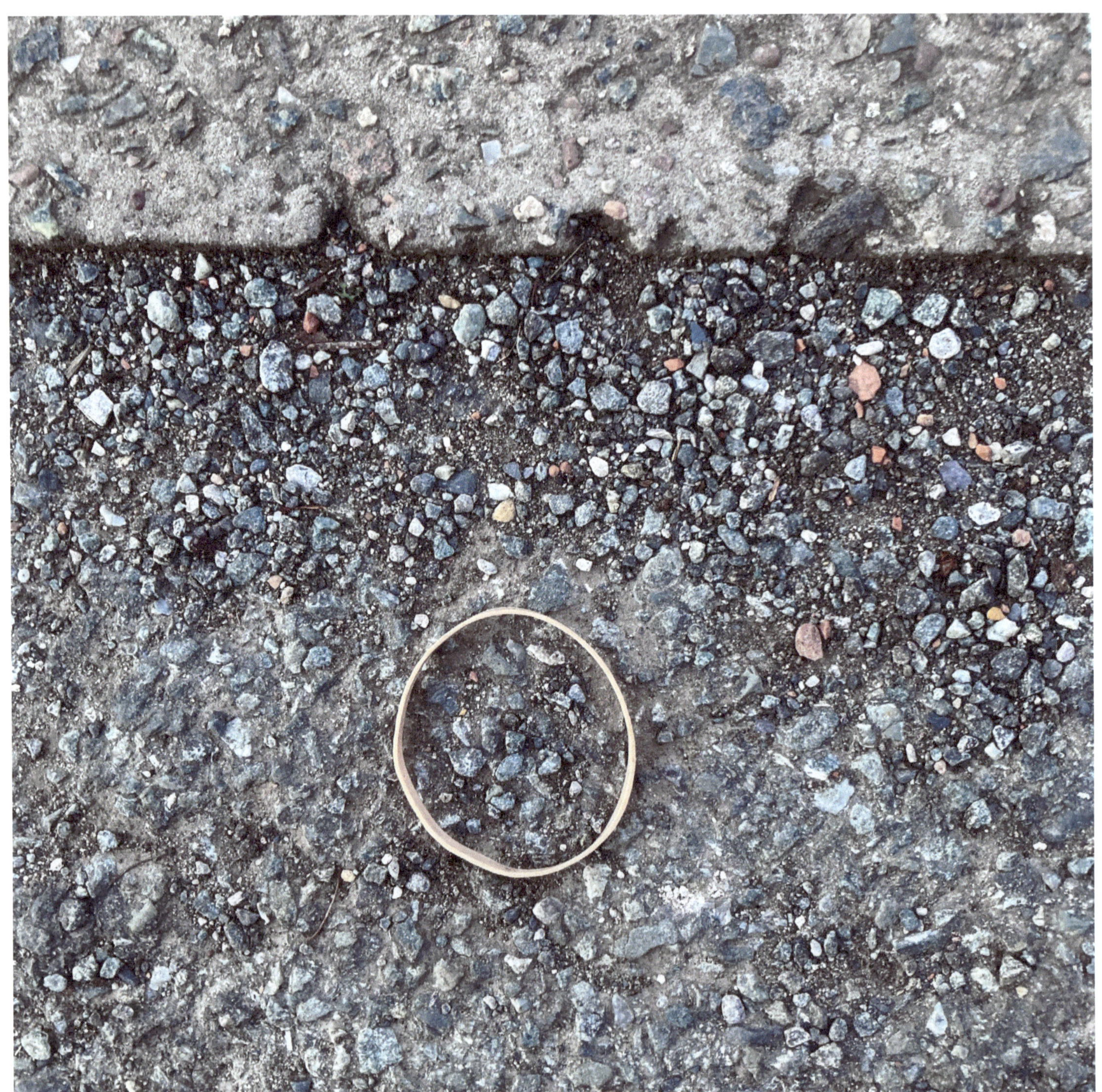

Band Below Two Caves

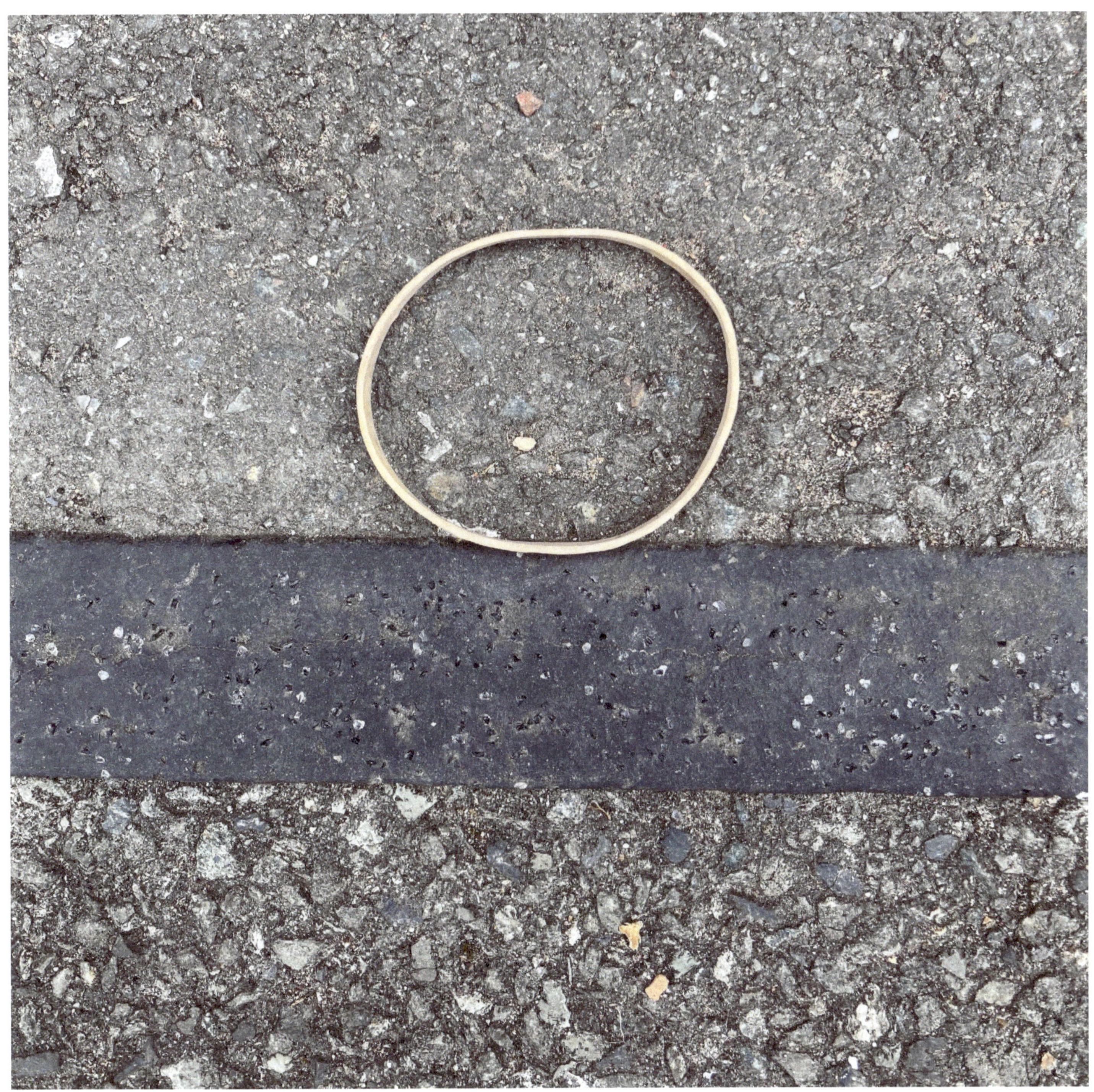

Black Under Grey with Circle

STRAWBERRY MOON

Tonight I imagine running
my tongue over the surface of you,
before tucking it back in my mouth
chalky dry.

Then I am picturing picking
sun-warmed sweet berries
for my replenishment.

Suddenly I hear her voice,
echoing from the past,
They'll know you ate some.

And I am paused
between those words
and the realisation that
my lips,
stained with the very joy of tasting,
are giving me away.

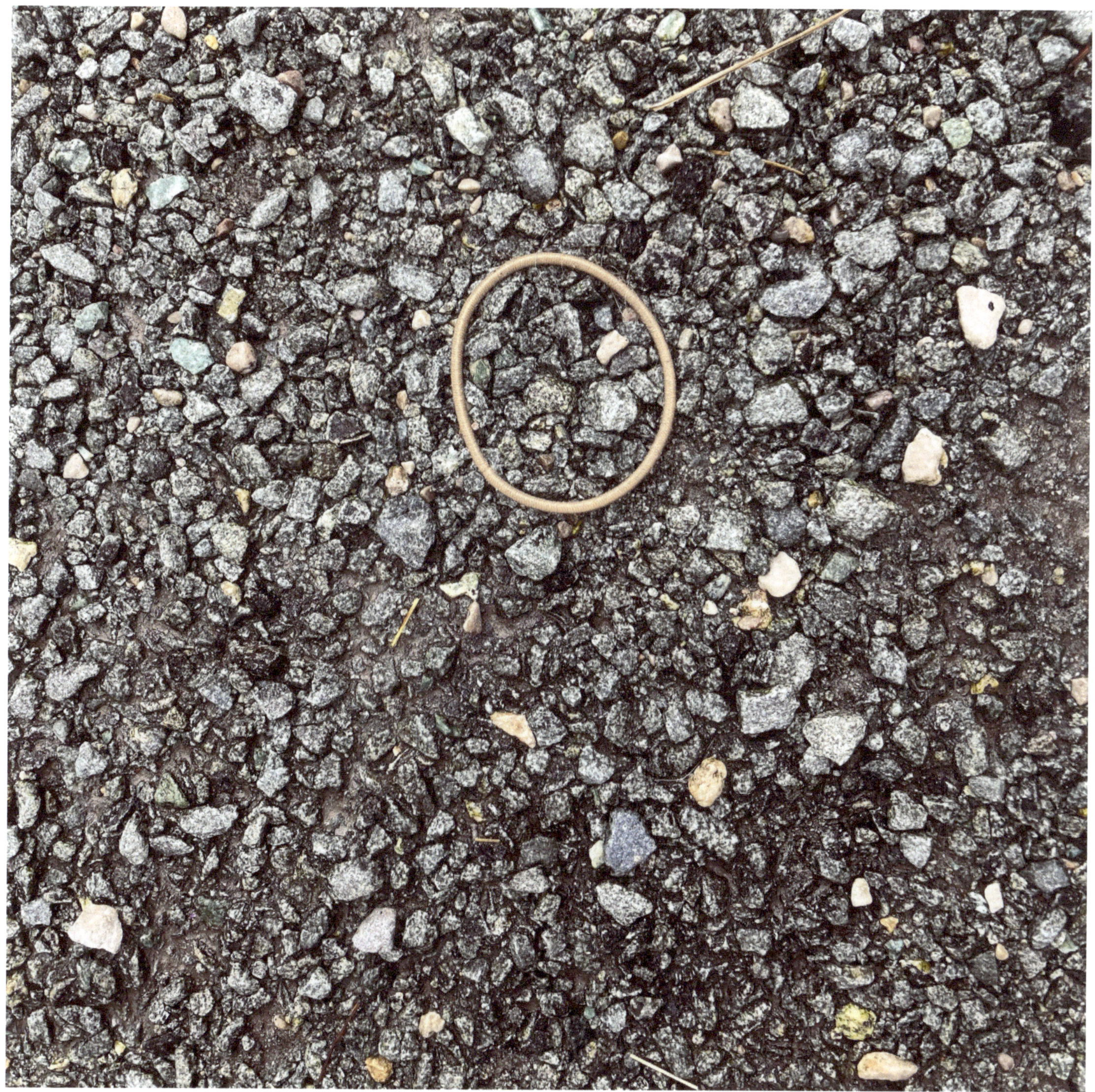

Great Orme

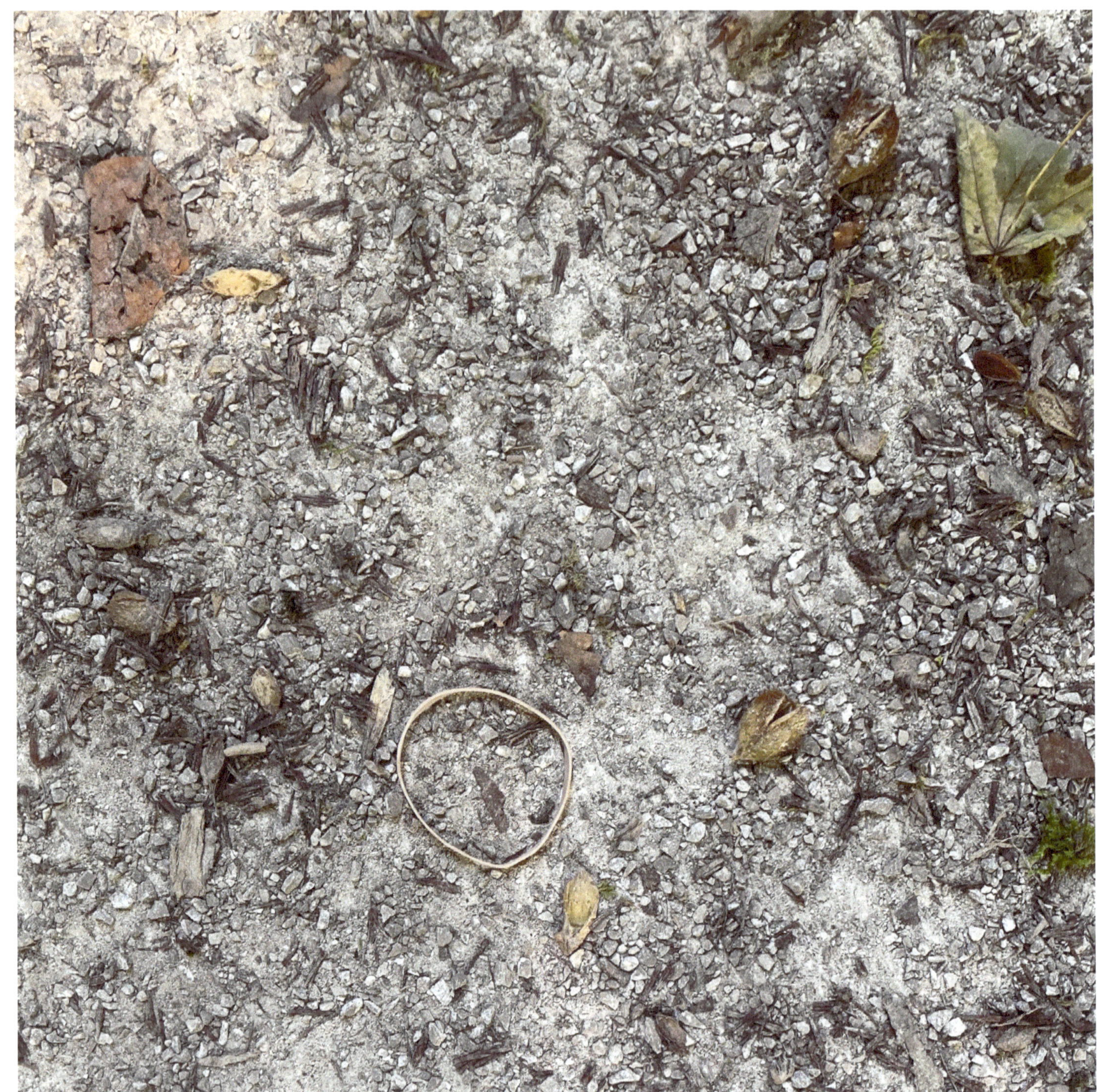

At Loggerheads

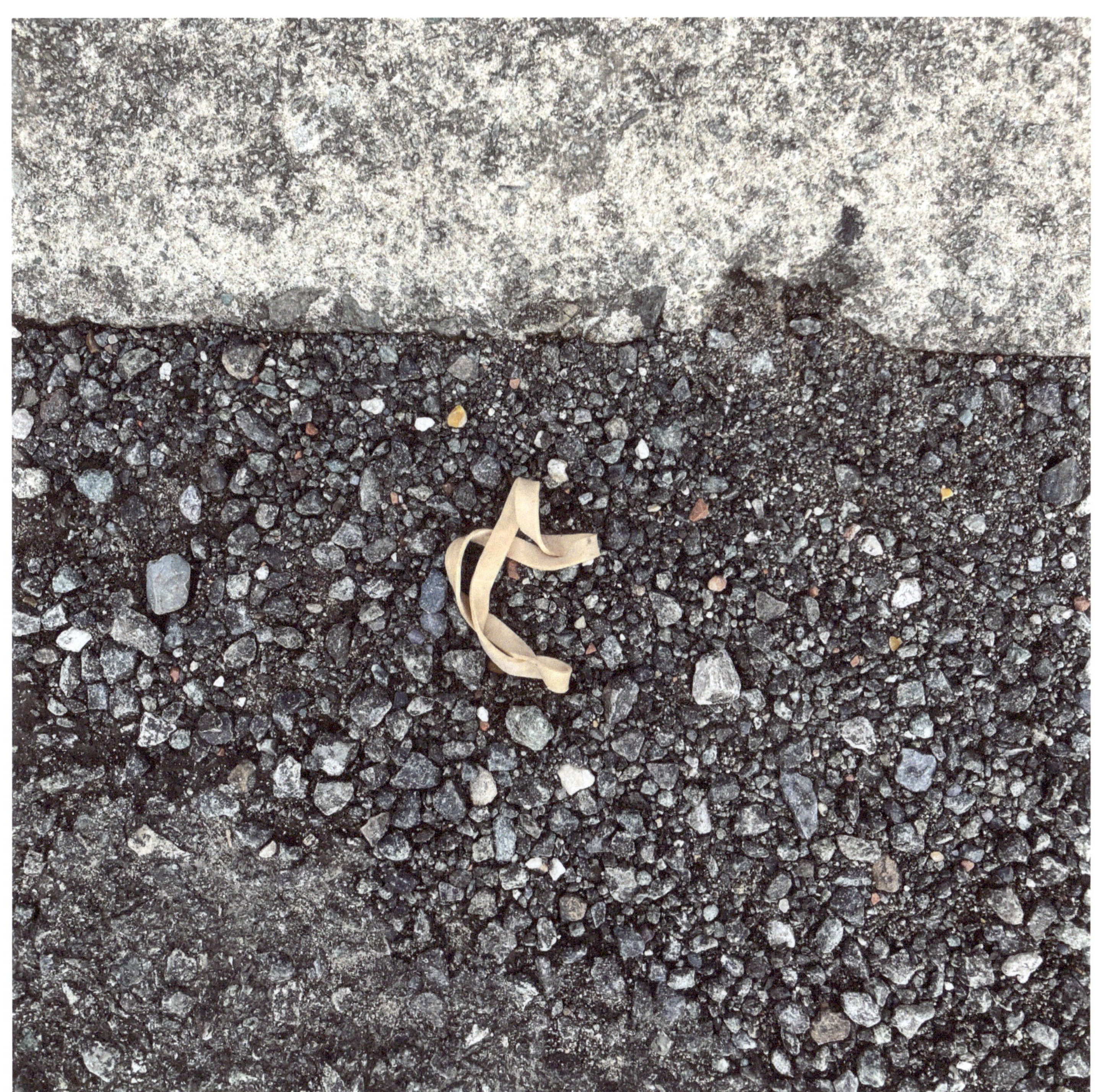

Jump

BUCK MOON: WHEN ANTLERS TANGLE
(Found in The New York Times)

Antlers exist for display.
Bones that start as nubs
sprout into sharp branches.

Days of summer pass
sheathed in fuzzy velvet.

By Autumn,
antlers will be ready
to posture,
preen,
lock horns.

False charges
avoid actual fighting,
but passions run high –

a buck with the head of another
tangled in its antlers. Twisted.
Complicated.

Unlock
or die through exhaustion,
starvation, thirst.

Animals battling near water
can fall in,
drown each other.

You may see locked up bucks
where one that's still alive
is watching the dead be eaten.

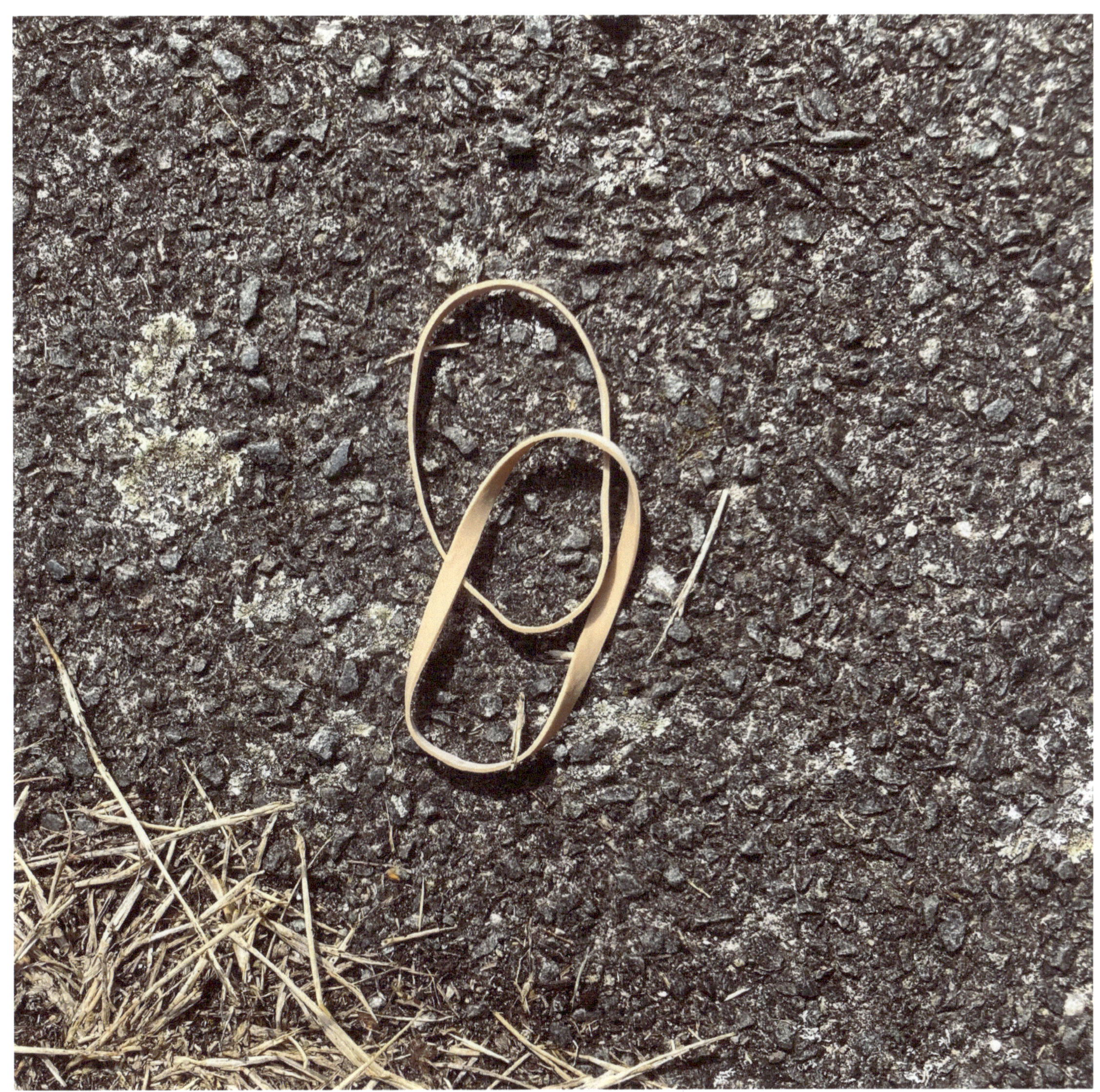

Double Up

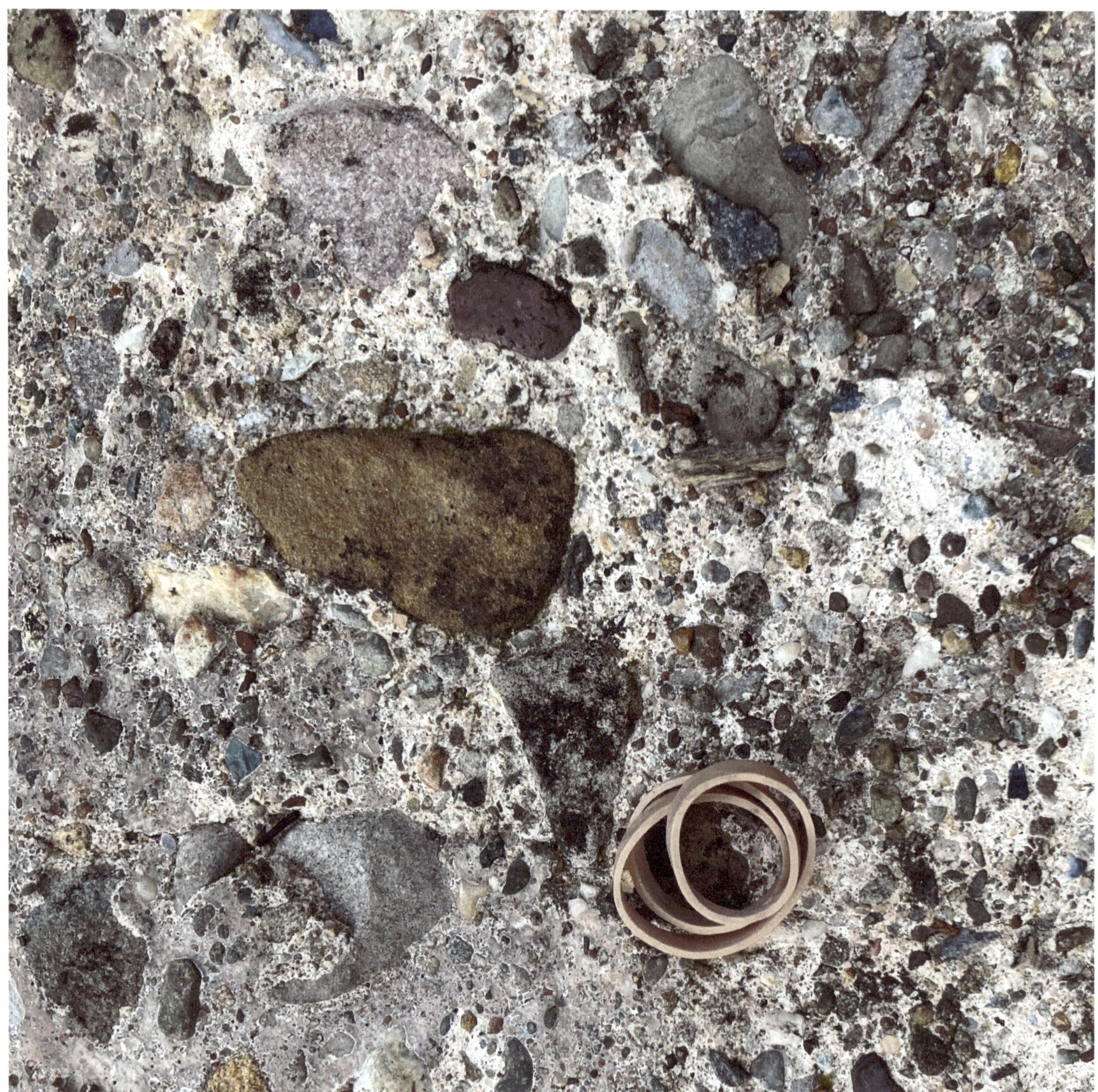

Vortex in Rubber

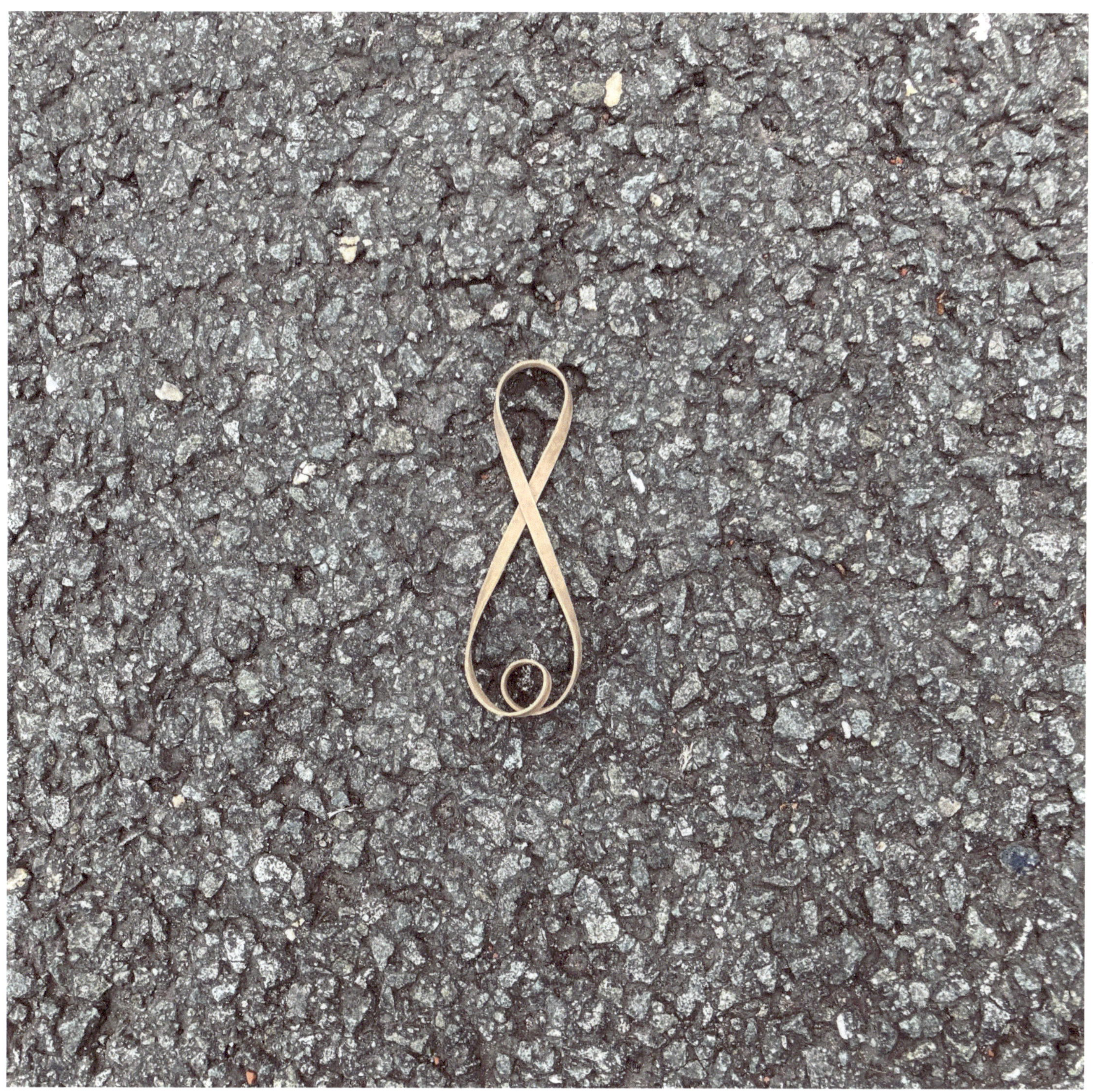

I Made This Shape For You

UNDER A STURGEON MOON

She is eating birds again
saving the heads till last.

She won't tell anyone
how much the feathers
in her stomach worry her.

Of all the reasons
sturgeon might leap
she hopes
it is simply for the feel of it.

She stands still in her own silence
waits for the splashes to reach her ears.

Another bird puffs
a last breath from its beak.

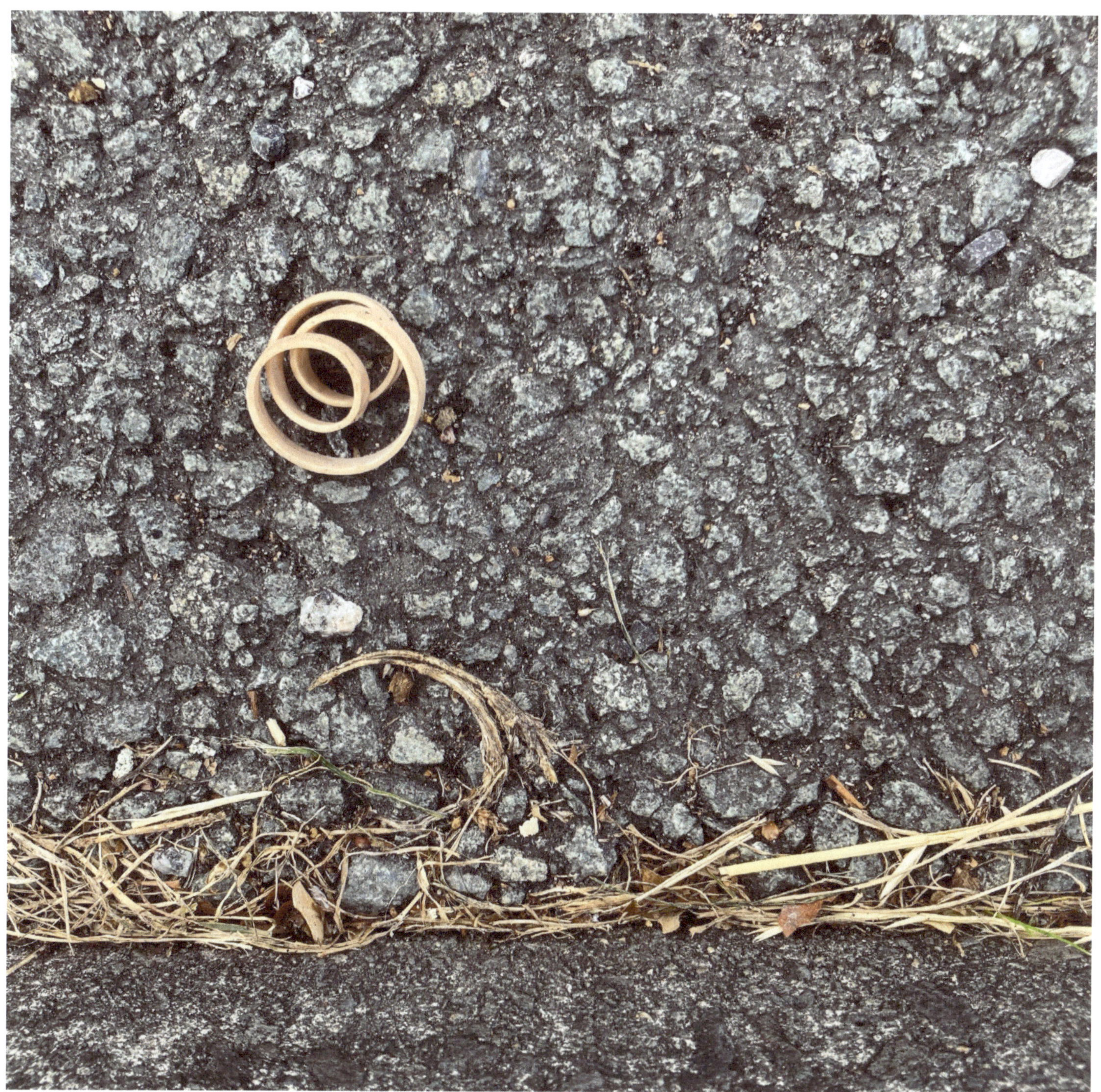

Vortex Over Wave

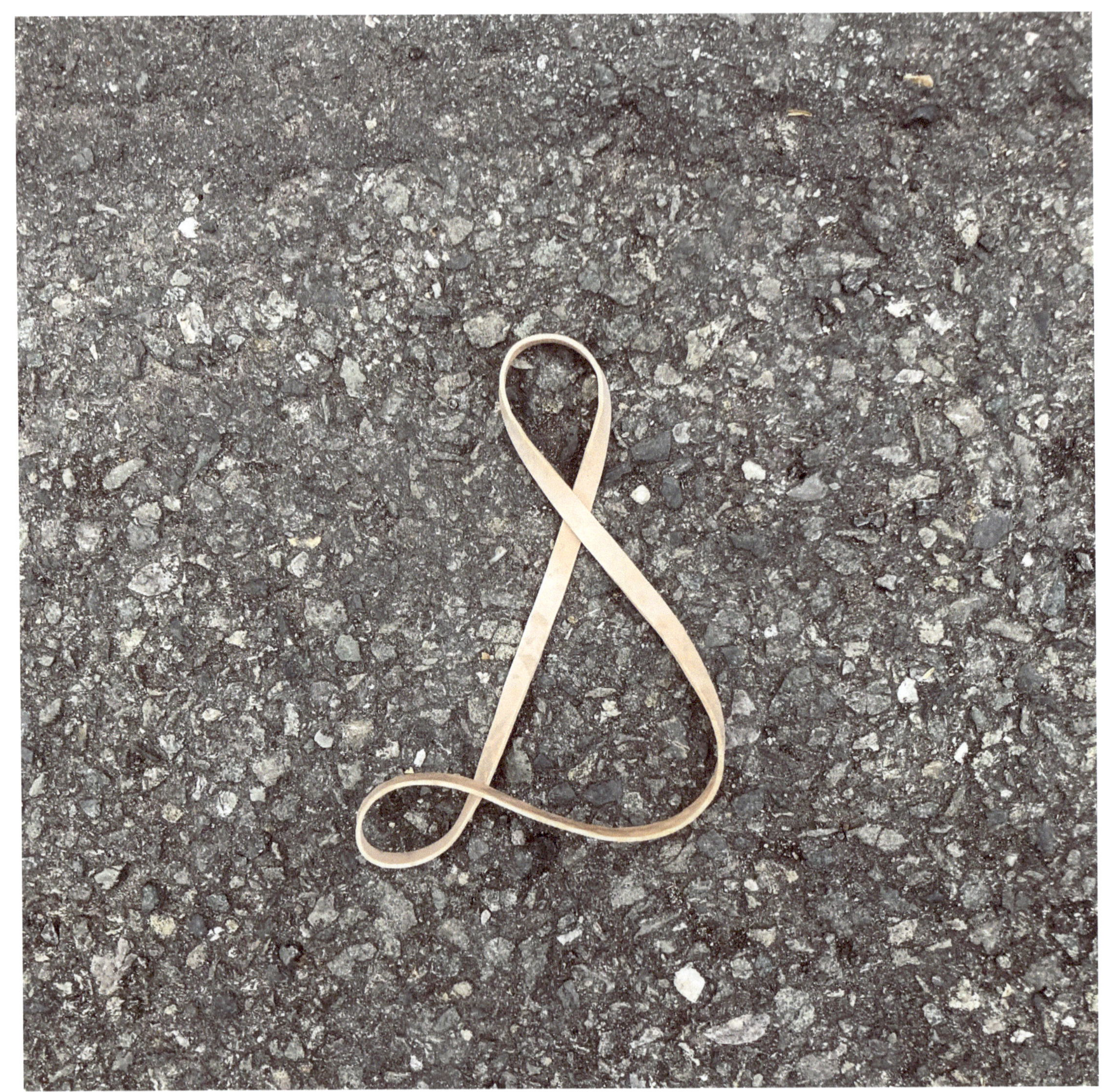

Ampersandesque

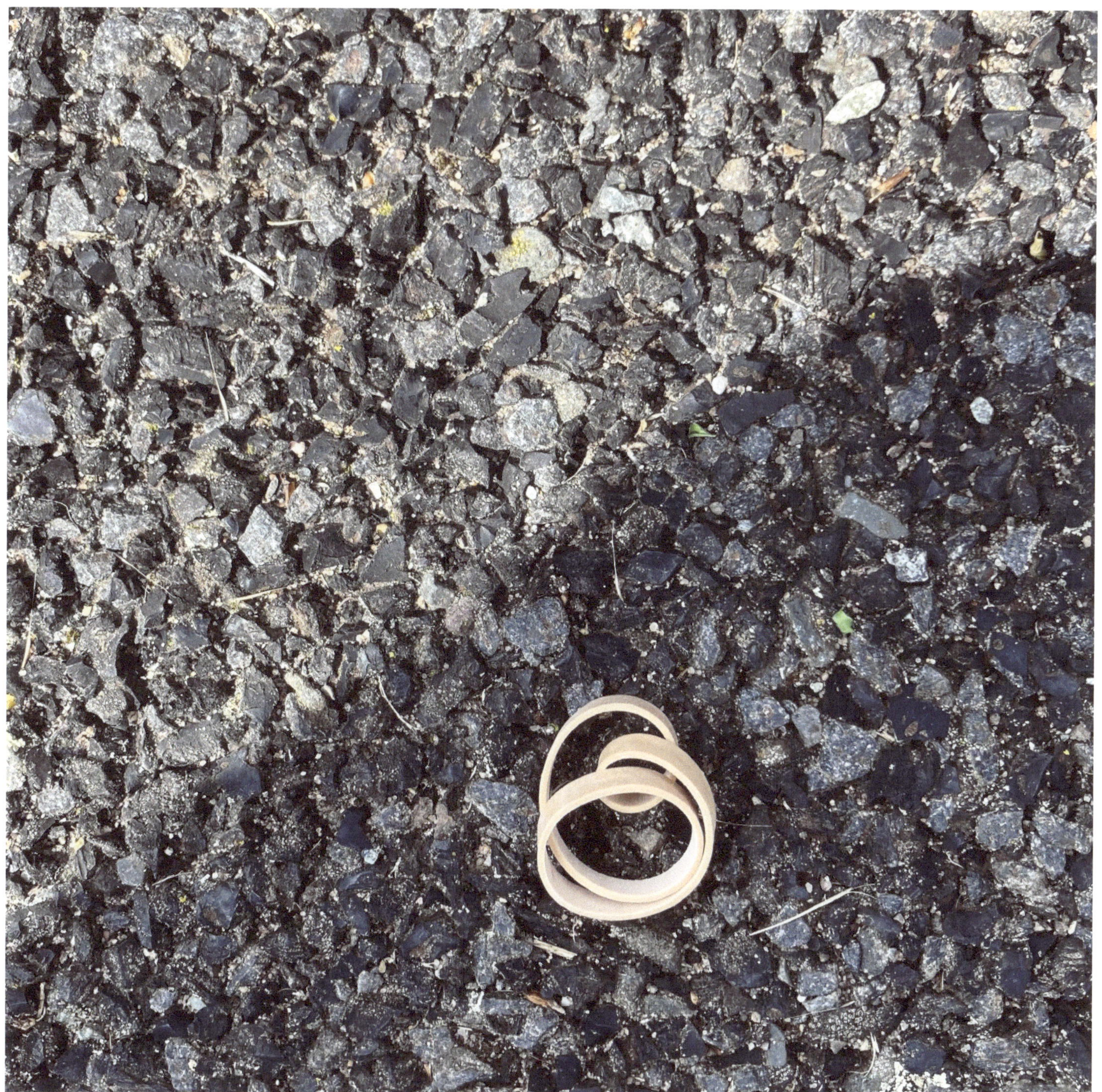

Curled in Shade

STOP EATING THE LOVE HEARTS

We scatter snow warmth,
swell soft gifts.

Thank you, thank you.

Near wayside evening birds,
more bread.

Thank you.

Then all our food gifts –
love hearts.

Refrain.

(N.B., this poem was found in the
traditional hymn 'We Plough the Fields
and Scatter' and after it was found it was
gifted its title.)

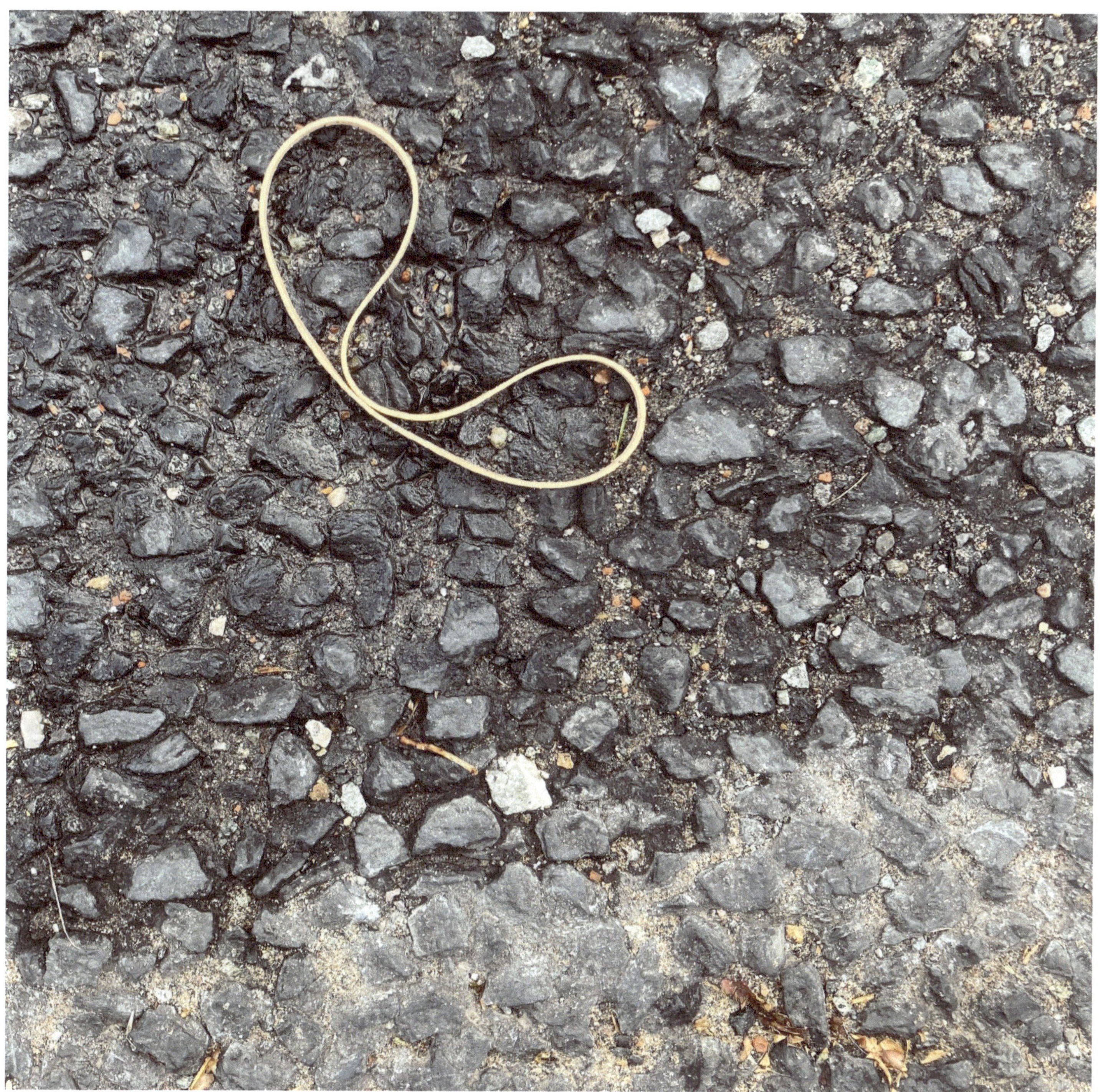

It's Probably For You

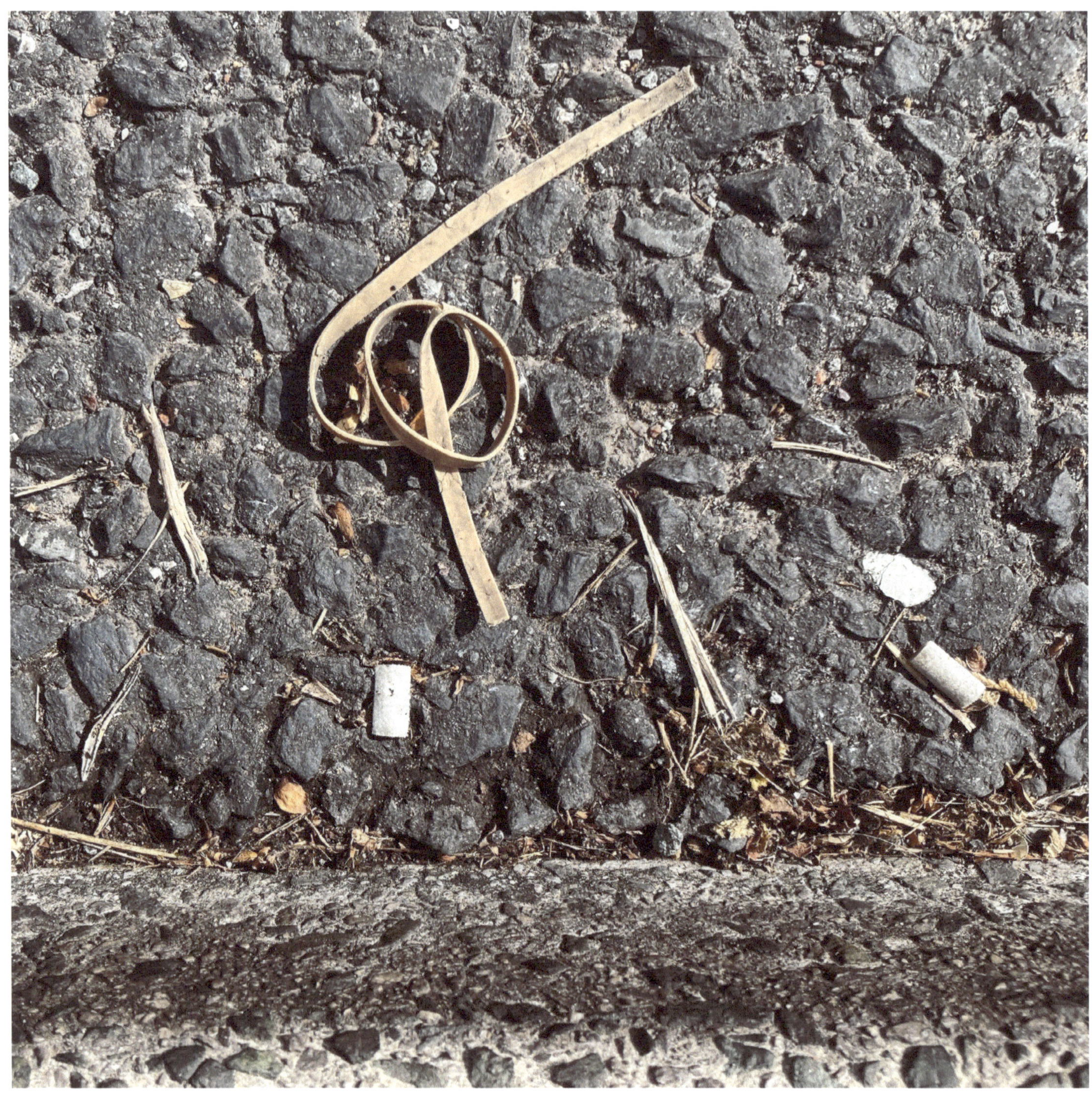

The Spin of the Pokemon Curveball

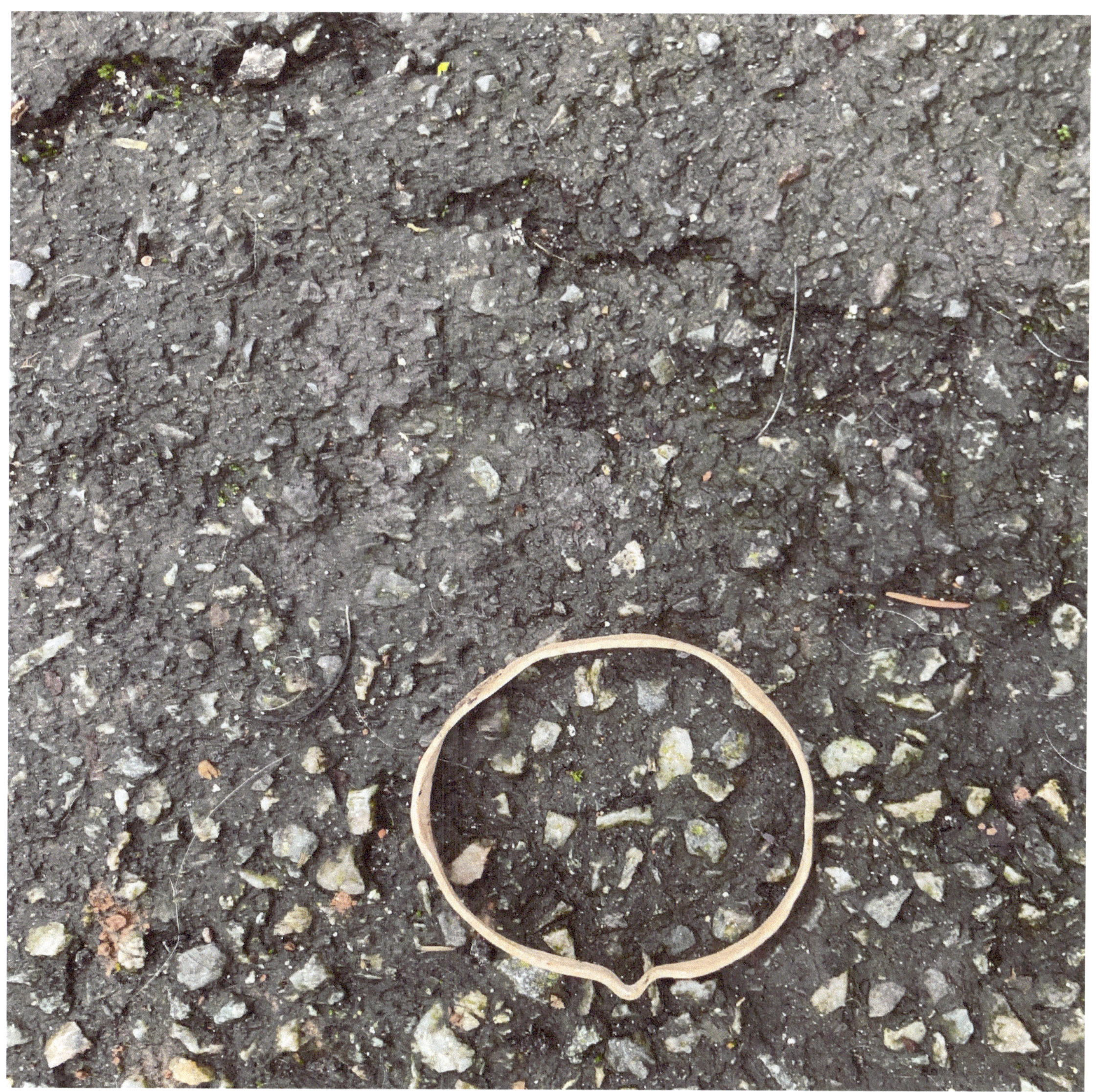

Let's Talk About the Way the Earth is Cracking

HUNTER'S MOON

The only thing I am hunting is you.

There is no secret, no real stealth.
I am blatant in my looking.

I love your light as the darkness says
it is creeping in.

I am holding you in reverence
as your circle fills
and I find you near my horizon
and then high above me.

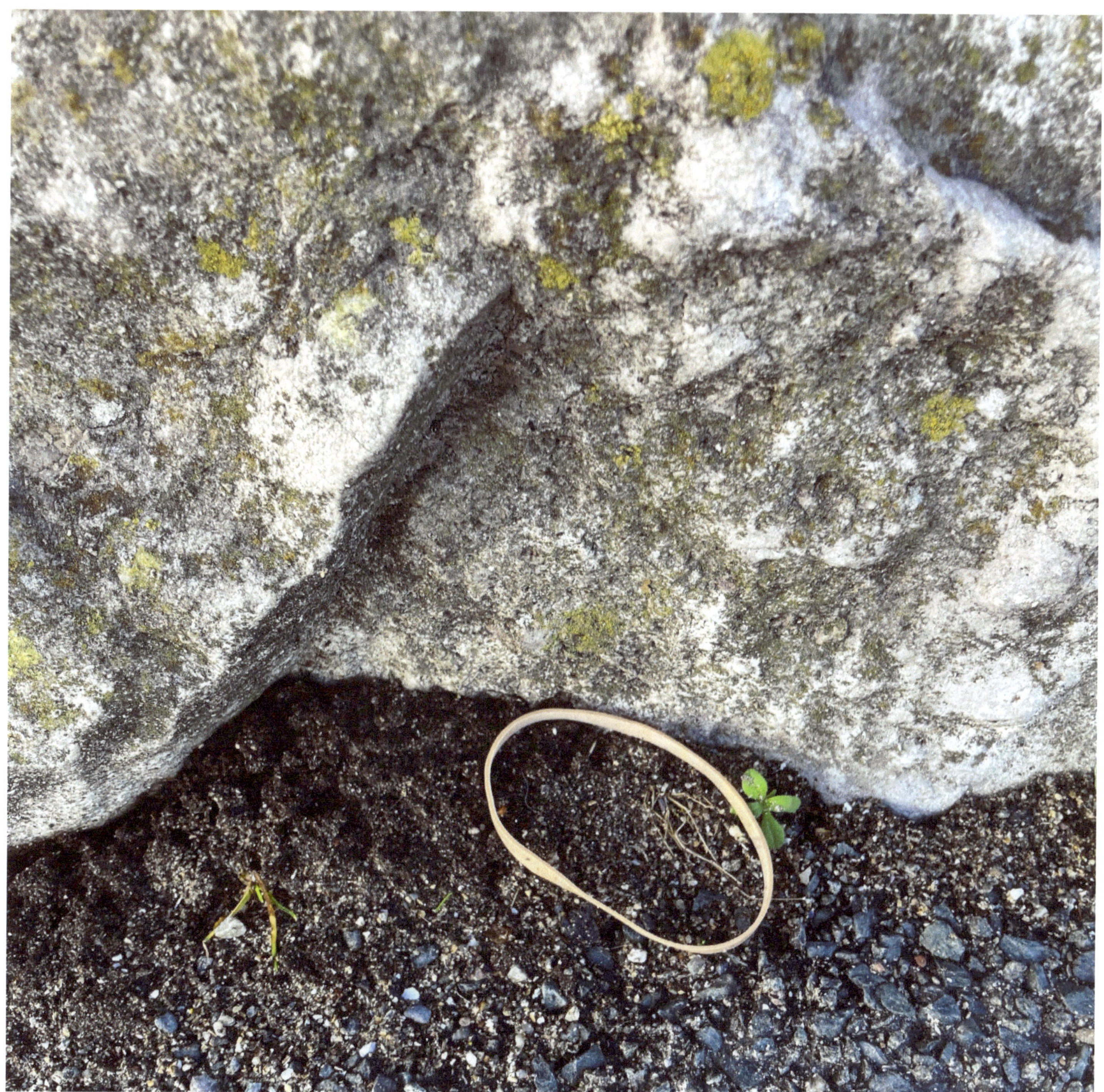

Potato Hoopla

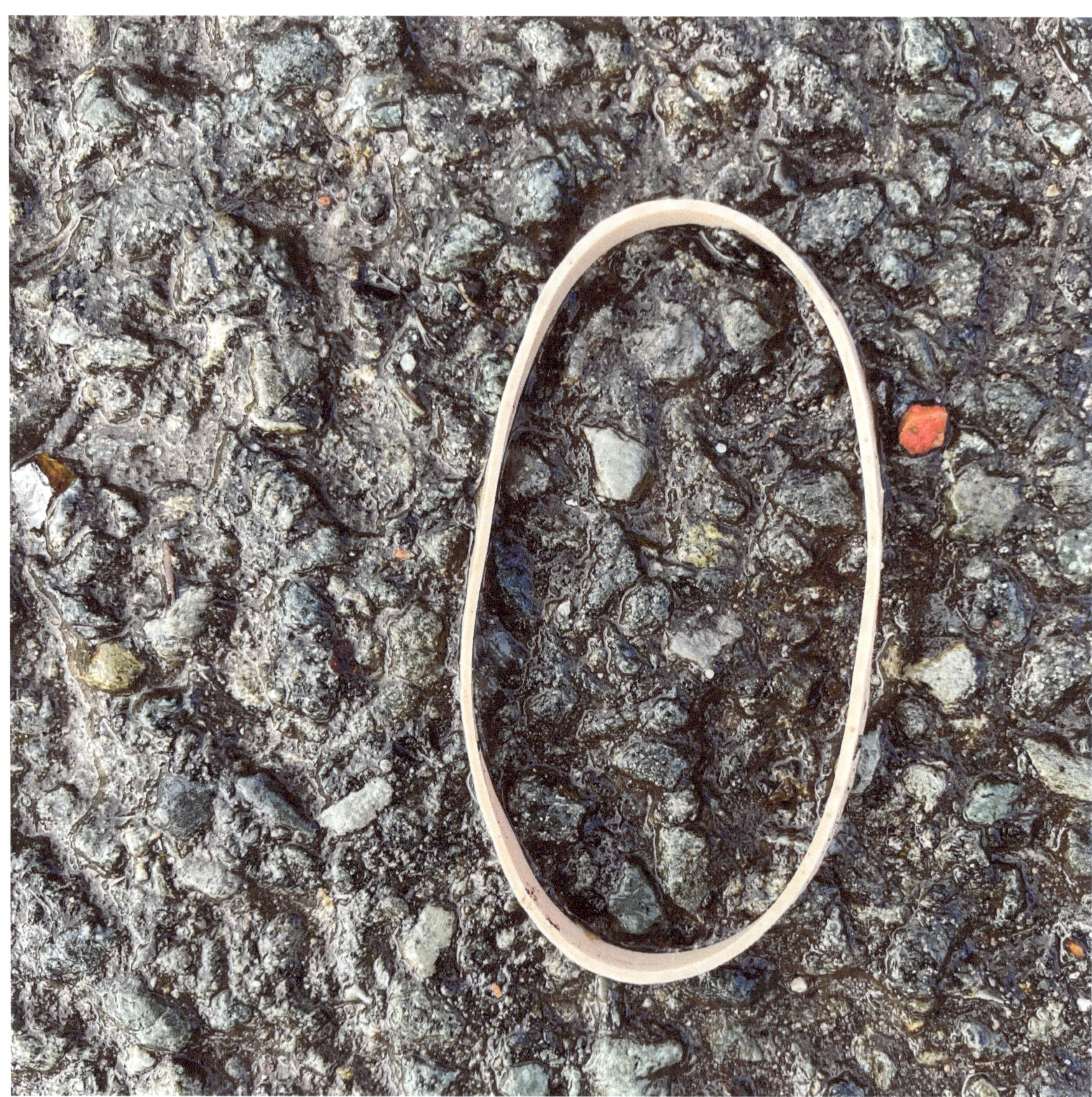

Red Eye (After Picasso)

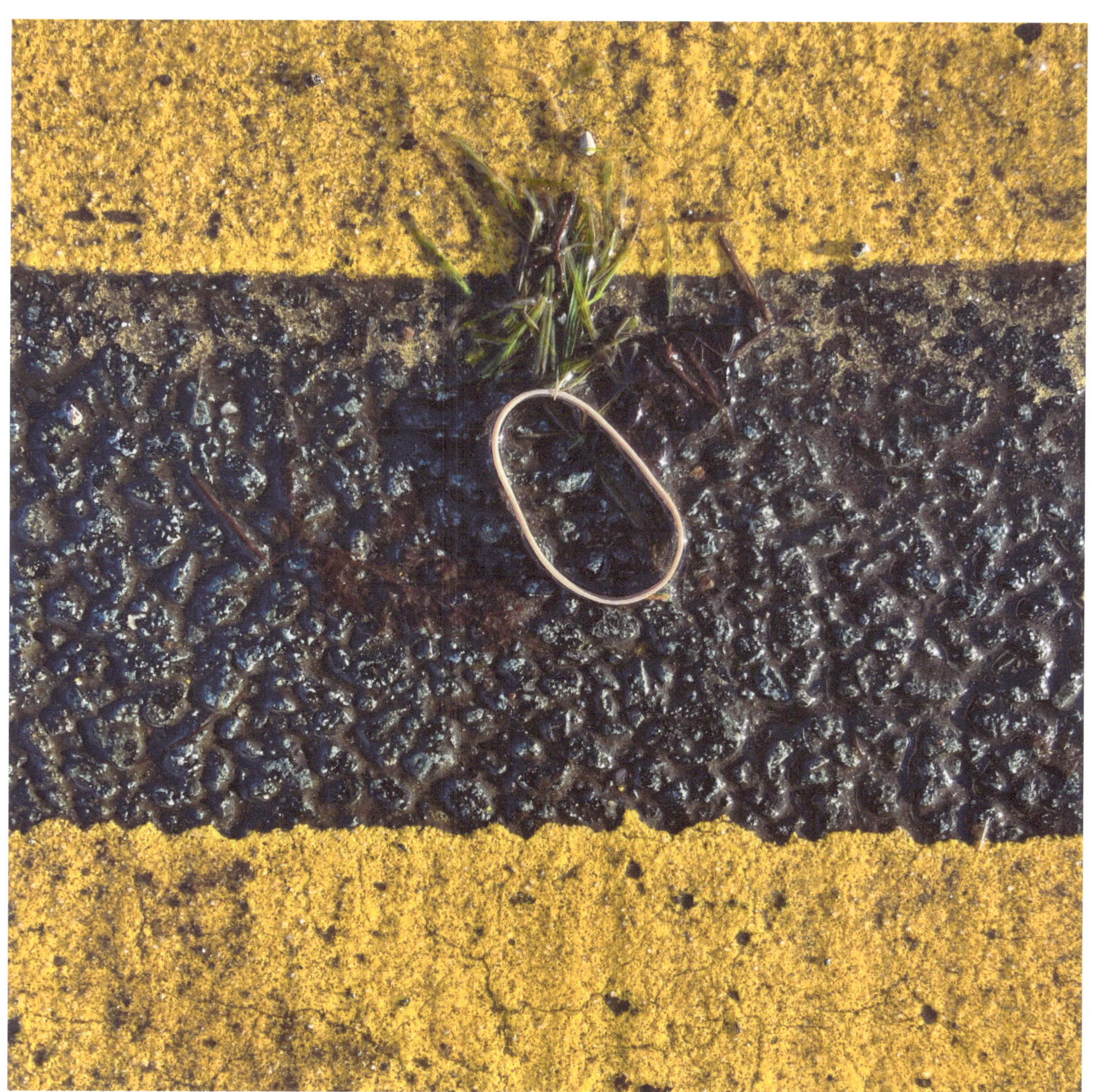

No Parking

BEAVER MOON

We stood under the sky
knowing the moon
would soon be full,
finding fireworks to match
those moments that have us breathless.

I told you that beavers are rodents –
the second largest after capybaras.
You said you didn't even know they were rodents.

I told you that my favourite firework
is the jellyfish that comes
after the Roman candles
which follow that rapid explosion
of rocket after rocket.

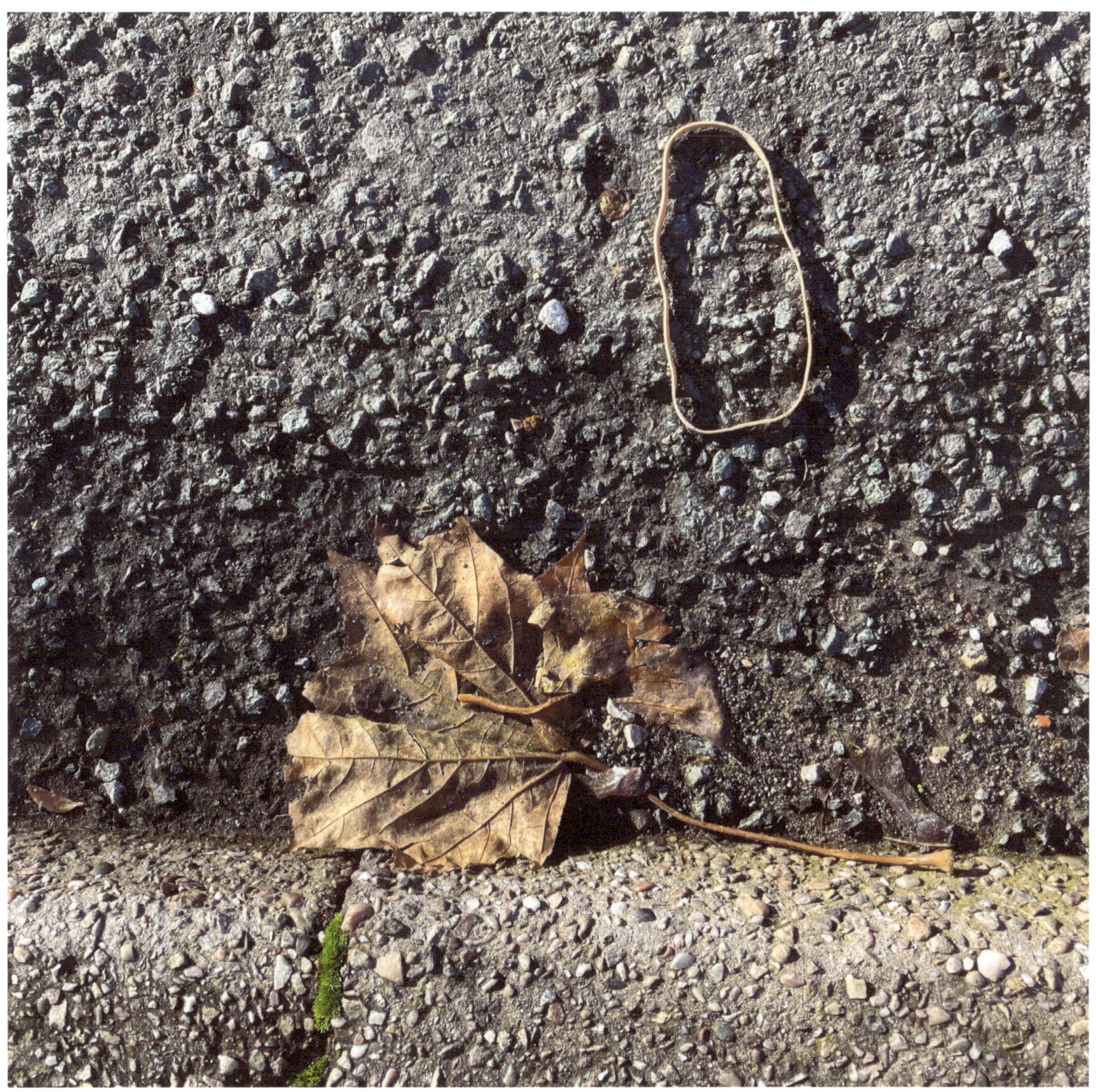

Leaf Under Matryoshka Moon

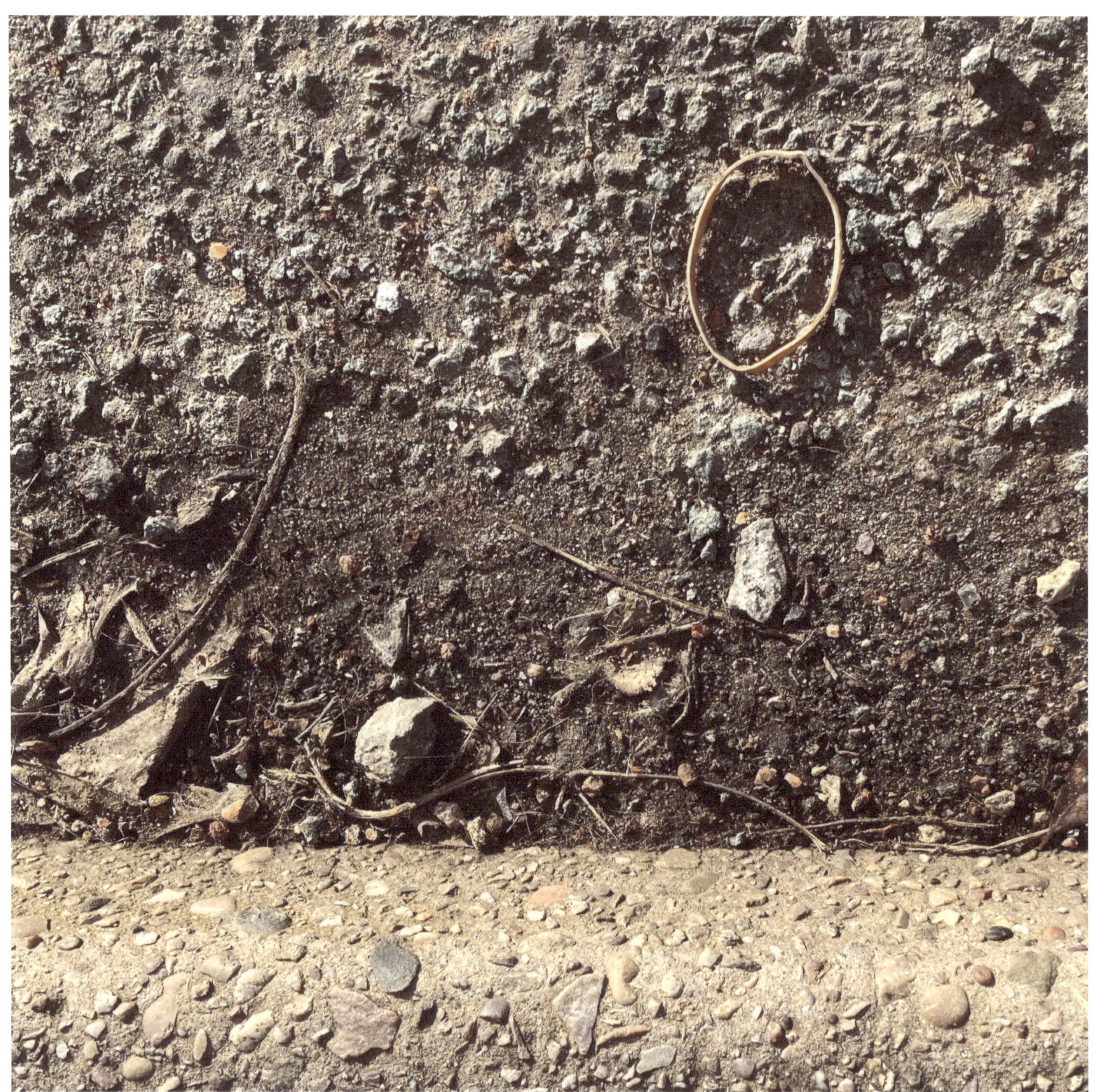

The Moon Rises and Time Sweeps On

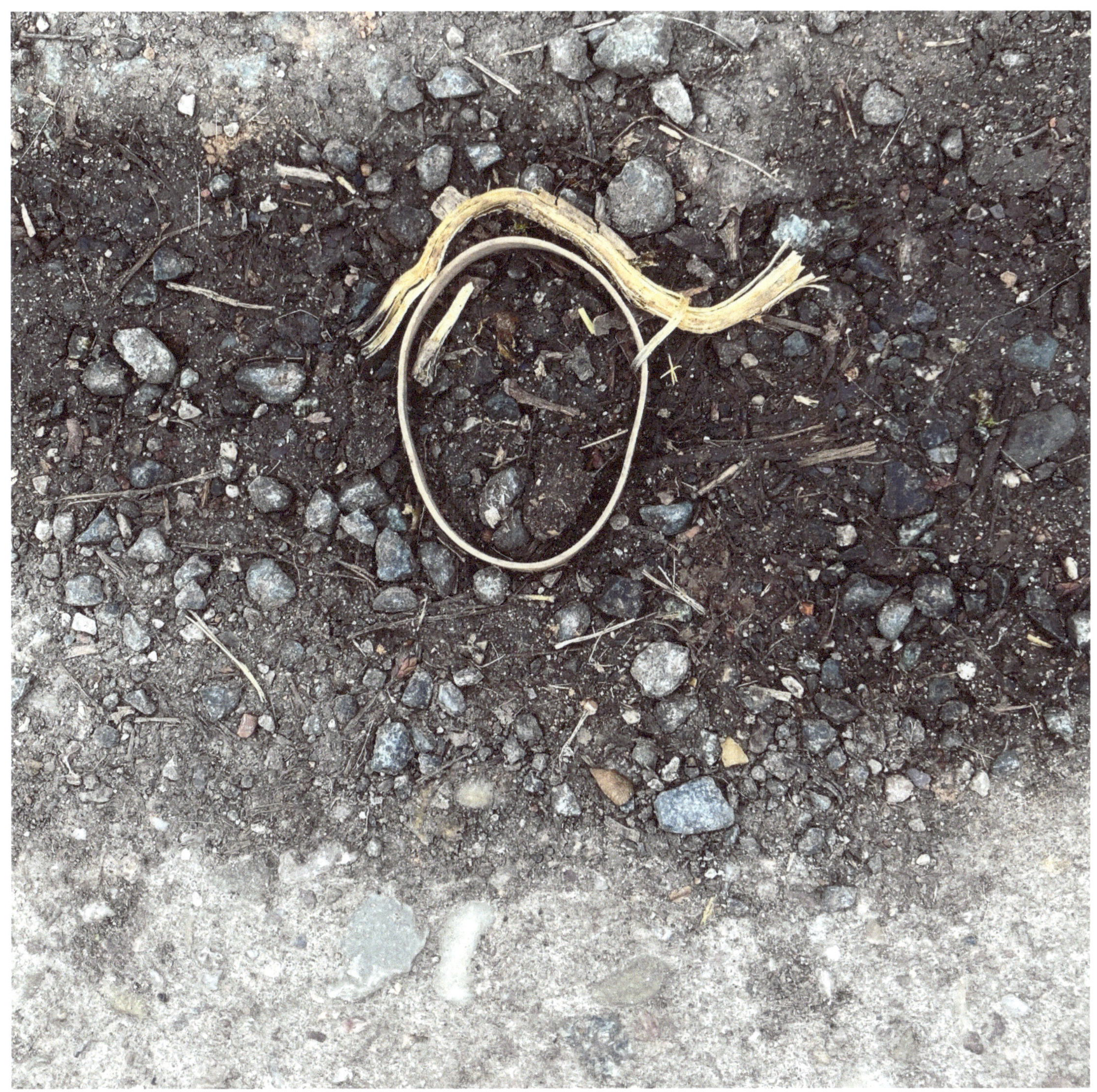

Do You Like My Hair Today?

COLD MOON

You were swelling
while I stood below you in Christmas lights
watching the clouds skim.

Cold under you now
I send out a wish on clouded breath.
Into the dark it goes;
an unruly puff
not the delicate smoke rings of birds that sing
on cold mornings.

Breathing in I feel
the rough shape of my lungs.

My timing says
I almost caught the perfect circle of you.

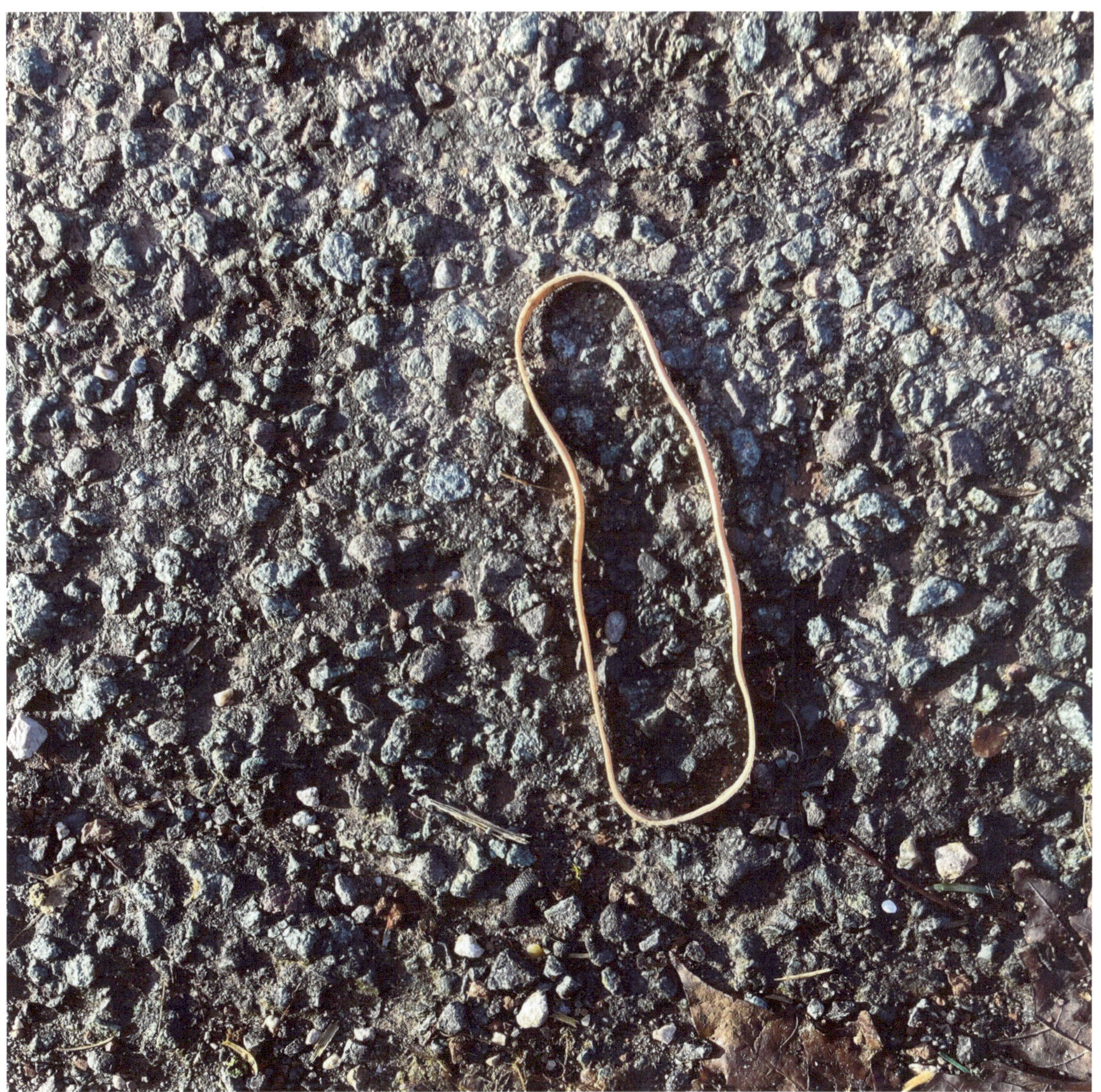

Outline of a Woman in Prayer

Fan Quotes

"Tell me there's going to be a book of these one day. It's exactly the sort of thing I'd leave out on my coffee table (if I had one) to impress guests (if I had any)."

Matt Quinn

"Lost an elastic band yesterday at Compton bay, Isle of Wight, if you fancy a trip."

Nina Parmenter

"I continue to love these band photos. They're so brilliantly inventive and reveal a beautiful way of seeing the ordinary things of the world."

Roger Hare

About the Author

Sue Finch likes all kinds of coasts, peculiar things, and the scent of ice-cream freezers. She lives with her wife in North Wales.

Sue won second prize in the 'Wild Words Single Poem Contest' in 2020 with 'Flamingo', a poem which then went on to be included in her debut collection, 'Magnifying Glass', and to be recorded for *iamb*.

Having been a regular participant in Top Tweet Tuesday, Sue was delighted to be shortlisted for the Dai Fry Award in 2022. Her work has appeared in several online magazines including: *Dear Reader, IceFloe Press, Ink, Sweat and Tears, One Hand Clapping* and *The Interpreter's House*.

Join the band...

Has this book sparked your imagination?
If you ever feel compelled to photograph
an elastic band that you spot on the
ground, let Sue know and consider writing
something as a response to it.

Be a litter hero!

Elastic bands can take over fifty years to degrade,
so the best option is to pick them up, where you
spot them, and reuse, repurpose or donate them to
your local school. Sue collects the bands she finds.

#ElasticBandPhotos

www.ingramcontent.com/pod-product-compliance
Lightning Source LLC
Chambersburg PA
CBHW042151030726
47599CB00004B/700